Praising *More for Less*

Wow! I was absolutely flabbergasted and I know you will be also after reading, *More for Less*. It challenges us to think and see things from God's perspective. Tyrone helps us to see the bigness of our God rather than the bigness of our problems. *More for Less* uniquely teaches and trains us to trust in God's ability to succeed and not our inability to fail.

I express my sincere gratitude to my natural and spiritual son for writing this book. I can proudly say, "Well done." I pray the Lord continues to use your wonderful gift of writing to enlighten and encourage the world at large. Above all, every chapter of this book reminds us again and again, truly "It's all about Him!"

BISHOP NATE HOLCOMB
THE CATHEDRAL OF CENTRAL TEXAS, CHRISTIAN HOUSE OF
PRAYER, COPPERAS COVE AND KILLEEN, TEXAS

This book has a heartfelt message, very uplifting and inspiring. As a writer myself, I must say that *More for Less* is a good read. This is a brilliant piece of work. I walked through the pages, stories, and examples and was reminded God can use even the least of us regardless of our past situations or shortcomings. It began pulling at my heart and inspired me to tell someone about it. I believe the insightful and inspiring stories in *More for Less* will empower people to achieve extraordinary success.

BISHOP DONNY BANKS
PRESIDING PRELATE, VICTORY GOSPEL CHAPEL,
SAN ANTONIO, TEXAS

In this book *More for Less*, the Holy Spirit uses Minister Tyrone Holcomb to demonstrate 1 Timothy 4:13. In his writings, Tyrone has been graced by God to give provision, encouragement, and instruction. When thinking about this God-given author, I am reminded of Acts 8:30–31.

More for Less will assist anyone in expelling the darkness of insignificance in their life and experience the light of God's love and grace.

PASTOR RODERICK MITCHELL
NEW LIFE CHURCH
CLEVELAND, MISSISSIPPI

Tyrone Holcomb is one of the most creative and prolific authors of our day. His insight, writing style, and presentation will keep you on your seat in expectation of what's ahead in the coming chapters. In the book *More for Less*, he goes beyond the common and traditional norm to inspire, instruct, and illuminate Christians on unlocking the more God has in store when you are dealing with less. The book will be a vital tool for every believer in pursuit of their divine design and for every person determined to fulfill their true destiny.

PASTOR JESSE GIDDENS
DESTINY CHRISTIAN CENTER
VICTORVILLE, CALIFORNIA

In today's world there are too many people who have discounted themselves and their usefulness in life. Ready to throw in the towel, they have resigned themselves to believe their own excuses for failure and relegated themselves to a place of insignificance. However, there is a promise in God's Word that He will give "beauty for ashes." This speaks of you as a better person, living in a much better place. But, promises can sometimes seem hollow without something practical to hold on to.

In this most recent book, you'll find practical wisdom and powerful tools to make God's promise of a beauty-filled life a reality for you. You may even begin to think Tyrone Holcomb was a fly on your wall and a thought in your head. So in his very unique way, he's describing your situation and giving you God's solution. Read it. Apply it. Share it. You'll be glad you did.

PASTOR ANTHONY WALLACE
CROSSROAD CHRISTIAN CHURCH
DOVER, DELAWARE

More for Less is a wonderful depiction of God's "Great Exchange." There are times when we all may feel inadequate, inexperienced, and incomplete for various reasons when it comes to the things of God and His selection of us for service. That type of thinking however automatically disqualifies us from receiving God's grace because it's not about our ability but our availability. I find this book to be a wonderful blueprint and source of encouragement and inspiration for those who have ever felt left back, left out, and even left behind.

DR. JOHNNY L. MAGEE, JR.
PASTOR/FOUNDER "THE HOUSE" CHURCH
VIRGINIA BEACH, VIRGINIA

Elder Tyrone Holcomb has done it again! He is a prolific writer. His writing style is not just inspiring but exciting. This book will cause you to anticipate reading every chapter with great expectation. His current book *More for Less* demonstrates the versatility and creativity he has to write intelligently on any subject.

In a time when people are struggling with self-promotion, Elder Tyrone reveals and pens the secret of life is not winning but allowing Him to win. This book is a must read for every person that is struggling to understand life's unsolved mysteries. Tyrone Holcomb not only provides information and inspiration but divine revelation into the plan and purpose that God has for our lives.

SENIOR PASTOR CARLOS KEITH
NEW HORIZON OUTREACH MINISTRY
NORTH AUGUSTA, SOUTH CAROLINA

More for Less is a book full of excuse-eliminating episodes of how trusting in God will turn our disabilities into possibilities. Tyrone helps us by not only sharing biblical truths, but also perfectly interjecting stories, including his own life's obstacles, to show us just how the Lord so wants to use us and help navigate us right into our purpose.

I believe *More for Less* is like a good bag of potato chips; once you start, you won't be able to put it down until you're done.

DR. ROBERT POOLE, JR.
PASTOR, DESTINY CHRISTIAN CENTER
LAS VEGAS, NEVADA

More for Less was written to help, inspire, and bring desire back to the young, old, handicapped, and even those who have lost their fire for the things of God! This book is a "must read," and it will truly encourage you to breakthrough and not breakdown. After reading this book, you will truly feel and understand what Jesus declared in Mark 9:23: "All things are possible to him who believes" (NKJV).

As I have heard it said before, this book will make a believer out of you! Even the unbeliever will not be able to deny that God can use anybody for His glory after reading this. The revelation through the natural principles here on earth to give us a kingdom understanding is priceless. I am a living witness that after you read this book, your disabilities can turn into possibilities!

PASTOR JAMES E. WILLIAMS
LIFE MORE ABUNDANTLY ISLAND CHURCH
WAHIAWA, HAWAII

Tyrone Holcomb is a masterful wordsmith. In *More for Less* he takes the content of thrilling though familiar Bible stories and recounts them in the context of our contemporary lives. He takes the Word of God and uses witticisms, quips, and memorable stories to make it relevant in the hard realities of everyday life.

This book equips the reader with eternal truths and practical wisdom. It is an engaging, easy read that inspires and motivates us to deal with the things that deal with us and empowers us to win.

EVANGELIST DOROTHY J. WHITE
FOUNDER AND PRESIDENT
GOD'S GLORY UNLIMITED INTERNATIONAL MINISTRIES
COPPERAS COVE, TEXAS

Lucille,
I pray the pages of this
book inspire you to trust God's
promises, power and presence
in the days ahead.
Much Love & Many blessings!
Myron "19"

TYRONE HOLCOMB

CREATION
HOUSE

MORE FOR LESS: TURNING DISABILITIES INTO POSSIBILITIES by
Tyrone Holcomb
Published by Creation House
A Charisma Media Company
600 Rinehart Road
Lake Mary, Florida 32746
www.charismamedia.com

Unless otherwise noted, all Scripture quotations are from the King
James Version of the Bible.

Scripture quotations marked NCV are from the Holy Bible, New
Century Version. Copyright © 1987, 1988, 1991 by Word Publishing,
Dallas, Texas 75039. Used by permission.

Scripture quotations marked NKJV are from the New King James
Version of the Bible. Copyright © 1979, 1980, 1982 by Thomas
Nelson, Inc., publishers. Used by permission.

Design Director: Justin Evans
Cover design by Judith McKittrick Wright

Library of Congress Control Number: 2016944690
International Standard Book Number: 978-1-62998-563-3
E-book International Standard Book Number: 978-1-62998-564-0

While the author has made every effort to provide accurate telephone
numbers and Internet addresses at the time of publication, neither the
publisher nor the author assumes any responsibility for errors or for
changes that occur after publication.

First edition

16 17 18 19 20— 987654321
Printed in Canada

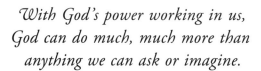

*With God's power working in us,
God can do much, much more than
anything we can ask or imagine.*

—EPHESIANS 3:20, NCV

Table of Contents

Introduction

Y EARS AGO I heard a story that bespeaks the very heart of this book. Allow me to share it in my own words. The beach waves lapped soothingly upon the shore. Sunbathers soaked up rays while children ran and played in the sand. All was calm on the beach front until the disturbing cries of a struggling man sent shockwaves throughout the atmosphere. As his struggle to stay afloat intensified, more and more attention was drawn to his plight.

Seeing the man struggle was of itself difficult to behold, but nothing could prepare the onlookers for what they'd see next.

Stationed nearby in an observation tower was the lifeguard, who appeared indifferent as he observed the man flailing about in the water. He didn't move a muscle, but gazed intently on the floundering man.

The fact that he didn't seem to grasp the immediacy of the situation, grab his rescue gear, and run to the water to save the man alarmed everyone. They began to yell at the lifeguard, beckoning him to do his job and save the man from sinking. It appeared the people's cries fell on deaf ears because the lifeguard was unmoved. Yet, his attention remained fixed on the drowning man.

The man in the ocean thrashed about vigorously in an attempt to save himself. His yells were desperate; his rescuer, distant. The people on the beach demanded the lifeguard act immediately; but he disregarded them entirely.

Finally, the man in the water stopped struggling. As the man went under the water, the lifeguard sprang into action. Equipment in hand, he swam to the drowning man and pulled him to shore. Once on shore the lifeguard administered emergency procedures to his victim and the man revived.

The onlookers were astonished. They demanded to know why the lifeguard waited to perform the rescue. The lifeguard reassured them of his experience. He revealed that waiting was the best course of action. He explained that while the man was fighting, his strength would have hindered the rescue. However, once the man became too weak to struggle, the lifeguard was able to save the man from dying.

This analogy is reminiscent of where many of God's people find themselves today. Some are struggling with stress while others are drowning in despair. Their countless cries for help reach the ears of God, but something halts the hand of God. Could it be like the drowning man; the Lord's hand is hindered from delivering the people who think they're strong enough to deliver themselves? It takes some of us longer than others to reach this conclusion, but eventually we all find ourselves at a breaking point. It is at this point we *give up* and He is able to *come down* with the requisite power to rescue and deliver.

The Apostle Paul learned God's grace is enough to get us through any test, temptation, and trouble. In fact, this Bible legend discovered God's strength is made perfect in our weakness (2 Cor. 12:9).

For this reason, He must increase and we must decrease

(John 3:30). In so doing, we will discover the inexhaustibility of God's power. And when our inadequacies surface, His limitless abilities come to the fore. In such times it is an exchanging of our inadequacy for His sufficiency, of our weakness for His strength, of our less for His more.

The bottom line is this: no matter where you are in life or what disadvantages present themselves to you, God's overwhelming desire is to turn your disabilities into His possibilities, to make your breaking point His breakout moment for you to break forth and fully experience your breakthrough.

It is my sincere desire that this book helps you receive God's *more* for your *less*.

I pray that the God who gives hope will fill you with much joy and peace while you trust in him.

—ROMANS 15:13, NCV

1

Hope for the Hopeless
God Is with Us

THERE ARE MANY reasons high school years can appear challenging. Making friends, learning subjects, and keeping up with trends are just a few obstacles the adolescent years present.

For me high school was simple with the exception of one particular subject—math. Honestly, math, and precisely *advanced algebra*, was the bane of my high school experience.

I vividly recall sitting in the rear of the classroom holding discussions that had nothing to do with figuring out the xyz's of any algebraic equation. My teacher would write formulas on the board that would leave Einstein scratching his head.

Known as the gregarious type, I would live up to my reputation with great alacrity. As I told stories that would make Mark Twain proud, my teacher would interrupt by saying, "Tyrone, pay attention or else!" Sure, I would pause long enough to receive his admonishment and then return to entertaining others who sat around me.

When my teacher could no longer stand my distractive

behavior, he would yell in a thundering voice, "Tyrone! I want you to answer this equation..." At that point the entire class was silent. I mean it was so quiet you could hear a feather drop on cotton.

As all the students stared in my direction, I searched my memory bank for answers only to discover it was insufficient. By this time I could hear giggles and whispers flowing from the amused onlookers. Suddenly my teacher repeated with a stern voice, "Tyrone! Give the answer to this equation..." The entire situation seemed hopeless.

What do you do when life seems to have you by the throat and won't let go? Where do you turn when you have more bills than money, your health is radically deteriorating, or a loved one decides they want to move on without you?

Hopelessness is the reality of so many. A man named Joseph found himself in a hopeless situation. His dreams were interrupted with the reality of deceit, devastation, and despair. Joseph's life is a lesson for the hopeless. His legacy inspires us to dream regardless of the circumstances and encourages us to never surrender to life's tragedies. The legacy of Joseph is found in Genesis, chapters 37 and 39–50.

Tragedy can strike quicker than my teacher could formulate an algebraic problem. However, every hopeless situation is brightened when we discover where to focus. When we are faced with problems, we must learn to look in the right direction.

DON'T LOOK AT YOURSELF

As a boy Joseph was his father's favorite son. The youngest of eleven boys, he received his father's affection in great profusion. It's likely the other boys had to settle for hand-me-downs, while Joseph wore garments tailored for his personality.

One piece of clothing that took on great significance was a coat hand stitched by Joseph's doting dad. The unique jacket was woven together with multiple fabrics and a kaleidoscope of colors. In essence, Joseph strutted around the neighborhood like a peacock spreading his feathers and the message was clear: "Look at me."

Joseph was groomed and pampered for a life of leisure, and this caused him to develop confidence. In fact, he began dreaming of a life where his family would serve him.

God desires for us to excel in life; however, He does not want our getting ahead to give us a big head. It's okay to have dreams and even better to accomplish them, but we are not to rely on our accomplishments alone. Scholastic degrees, talents, and charisma are good attributes, but not enough to secure true satisfaction.

Looking only to ourselves for satisfaction or fulfillment could lead us to a dark and lonely place. Joseph was innocent with well-meaning motives, but he was forced to learn a difficult lesson. He had to discover he could not depend solely on his own ability nor rely entirely on the strength of others.

Don't Look at Others

Being younger than his ten brothers could have left Joseph with a sense of tenacity. Then again, he could have also developed a dependency on his older siblings. After all, he did dream they would become subservient to him.

If the latter held true and Joseph did depend on his brothers, he was in for a rude awakening. Joseph's brothers despised him and searched for every opportunity to rid themselves of his presence. Oddly enough, Joseph seemed clueless to his brother's animosity.

One day he was sent to locate his brothers at his father's

beckoning. At last he discovered there whereabouts and as he approached them they conspired against him. Their collusion toward their brother would set in motion an arduous journey that would alter the course of Joseph's life.

When Joseph reached his brothers, they took hold of him and ripped away his unique coat of many colors. They began to push and pull, taunt and tear at him and finally, they dropped him in a dark pit. There was young Joseph battered and beaten by the very brothers he looked to for provision and protection.

For the first time Joseph found himself hopeless. He cried out to his brothers for attention and assistance, but they ignored his screeching pleas. This belligerent bunch ate a meal while their younger brother lay just feet away in a pit of despair.

Soon after, Joseph's brothers sold him. The young man who had dreams of being great was bartered like merchandise. When Joseph thought he could count on his brothers, they were off counting the coins they gained at his expense. Joseph's brothers were not the only ones to let him down.

As an Egyptian slave, Joseph worked long and diligently for his master. Although he was subjugated, Joseph caused prosperity to come to this man's entire estate. It wasn't home, but Joseph learned to make the best of a bad situation.

Joseph had settled into his new life, he gained favor with his master, and he was promoted as overseer of the other servants. Just when it seemed his future beamed bright with potential, his master's wife sexually harassed him.

Out of loyalty to his superior, Joseph rejected her adulterous advancements; and out of rage, she accused him of attempted rape. And just like that, Joseph's new life, new home, new position came to an abrupt end. When his master returned home and heard the spurious tale his wife concocted about Joseph, he had no choice but to have Joseph imprisoned.

Once again, the young Hebrew found himself in a hopeless situation. Once again, the people he looked to do him right had done him wrong. Joseph was thrown into a pit by his brothers and tossed into a prison by his master. However, even in the prison this man's potential was obvious.

The old adage, "You can't keep a good man down," was certainly true about Joseph. This man experienced more than his share of letdowns, but to hold him down was proven difficult. Even in the dungeons of Egypt, Joseph showed himself resourceful. Thus, he was given charge over all the other inmates.

As time passed, Joseph met the king of Egypt's butler. This man was depressed because of a dream he had the night before. Ironically, Joseph, who was put in a hopeless situation, looked to encourage and restore the butler's hope. Joseph interpreted the man's dream and revealed that he would be reinstated to his position as the Pharaoh's butler.

Joseph told the butler how he was stolen from his beloved father and sold as a slave. He went on to say how he was wrongly accused and thrown into prison. He asked the butler to mention his terrible plight to the Pharaoh hoping to be released. Elated to hear of his own pending fortune, the butler promised he would speak on Joseph's behalf.

According to Joseph's interpretation, the butler was released and restored to his dignity and duties. However, contrary to his promise, the butler forgot all about his comforting companion. As Joseph eagerly waited for news of his release, days became weeks, weeks became months, months became years, and once again his hopes went unfulfilled.

Joseph looked to his brothers and was despised; he looked

to his Egyptian masters and found disloyalty; and he looked to the butler and discovered disappointment. When it seemed all was lost, in his darkest moments Joseph realized he was looking in the wrong direction. He finally figured out his hope would not come from himself or others, his hope was found only in his God.

Beloved, where are you right now? Are you the subject of ridicule? Are you facing impossible odds? Has someone let you down? More importantly, are you at the end of your rope and low on hope? If the answer to any of these questions is yes, then learn to look up, not around. Discover what Joseph figured out—God is in control.

Look to the Living God

If we were to recapture the negative accounts of Joseph's life, we would unearth a common thread—God was with Joseph.

As a young boy searching for his brothers, Joseph encountered a certain man who told Joseph the location of his brothers. Who was this man? The Bible does not reveal this man's identity, but we can trust this man was there according to God's divine plan (see Genesis 37:15–17).

In the days when Joseph was captive and serving his Egyptian master, the Bible records, "The LORD was with Joseph" (Gen. 39:2). At the time when his master's wife accused him of obscene behavior and had him wrongfully thrown in prison, the Bible emphatically states, "The LORD was with Joseph" (v. 21). The Lord was with Joseph when he interpreted the butler's dream, yet in all these instances Joseph's life seemed to be spiraling in despair.

Have you ever felt that way? Does it appear no matter how you live right and serve the Lord you're always left with the short end of the stick? If so, don't despair; even in the tough times, no, especially in the tough times, the Lord is with you. He's with you when others leave you; He's with you when the malignant disease attacks your body; He's with you at your greatest loss.

It's a conundrum unparalleled to any other, how in the presence of God there could be so much pain. However, isn't it reassuring? This world brings problems, pain, and pressure; but through it all, it's wonderful to know our God is with us.

God is the peace in the eye of our storms. We are not to consider our own strength or the strength of others; we must depend only on the might of the Lord. God never promised we wouldn't have problems; He promised to be the answer (Rom. 10:13). The truth of the matter is, we'll never discover God is all we need until He is all we have. This was the lesson Joseph had to learn.

The day finally arrived when Joseph was called upon to aid the Pharaoh, ruler of the vast regions. The Pharaoh requested Joseph's interpretation of his dreams and Joseph's response changed the course of his life. He went from bad, good, and into God's very best by simply stating, "[The answer] is not in me: God will give Pharaoh an answer of peace" (Gen. 41:16, NKJV).

Joseph learned to look to the living God and cause others to look to the Lord as well. For us to look toward God means going beyond being delivered to becoming developed. We must comprehend what Joseph figured out: the evil others intend for our detriment; God works for our benefit (Gen. 50:20). The devil tempts to bring out our worst; however, God tests us to bring out our best.

Do you remember the account in my advanced algebra class? I was being a disruption so my teacher decided to ask me to solve the equation.

All eyes were glued to me as I struggled to give the solution. Suddenly, I heard a small reassuring voice whispering the answer behind me. I verbally submitted the answer I was given, and to my surprise the answer was correct. Later, I discovered the voice came from a young lady who sat directly behind me.

Some weeks later I was in the same class again holding independent conversations in the rear of the room. And once again I was placed on the hot seat to solve an algebra problem. However, this time I noticed I had not sat in the same seat as before. Therefore, I felt without hope when suddenly I heard the same reassuring voice whispering the answer. Amazingly, the same young lady had again situated herself behind me. I gave the teacher the answer and again it was correct.

This time after class I approached the young lady to thank her for the assistance. I further asked why she gave me the answers and even changed her seat. I smiled when she replied she liked me.

Remarkably the Bible records that God is always behind us to give the answers (Isa. 30:20–21). Allow my example and Joseph's life to sound one blatant truth: when we're faced with tests and troubled on every side, God is with us.

God is with us for one earthshaking reason. Do you know why? Some think it's because of their undying devotion to Him; others believe it's their good works for Him. Even still, many consider their good behavior the cause. These are all good reasons, but not the right reasons.

God is with us because He likes us! His liking us—even loving us, has nothing to do with us and everything to do with Him. He's just wired that way. God is love! (1 John 4:8).

Remember, God will turn your disability into His possibility because He is the *hope* for the hopeless!

Chapter 1
POINTS TO PONDER

When you're faced with problems, where should you focus: yourself, others, or God?

_____

The biblical patriarch Joseph's life should be a lesson in what way?

_____

_____

How can depending on your accomplishments hurt you?

_____

_____

Has someone disappointed you? If so, how did you handle the let down?

_____

_____

Are you over the disappointment? _____

Have you given the matter to God? _____

Can you look back and see God was with you in your problems? If so, explain:

_____

_____

_____

Are you looking for deliverance or development?

_____

Lord, because I am poor and helpless, please remember me. You are my helper and savior. My God, do not wait.

—PSALM 40:17, NCV

2

Help for the Helpless
The Process to Progress

S OME YEARS AGO I bought a new Blu-ray player for my
television. When I returned home with it, I wasted no
time. I tore into the box, bypassed the instructions, and
proceeded to power up my new toy.

Andrea asked if I needed help. I just smiled in her direction
and replied, "No thank you." Her offer to help was appreciated but unnecessary, because I had everything under control
(so I thought).

When it came time to program and operate the various
functions and features of this gadget, it didn't make any sense.
I tried reading the instructions, but the writing appeared to
be coded language that da Vinci couldn't decrypt.

After a few hours, I finally conceded to the unthinkable—I
needed help. As much as it injured my ego, I decided only one
course of action was in order. With my manhood wounded,
I called my wife's name, "Andrea—Andrea!" Fortunately, my
cries for help were heard.

Andrea emerged from her activities to assist. She made an

attempt to grab the remote to the Blu-ray player from my hand, but I pulled away. She made yet another attempt and I persisted to resist.

With pity Andrea asked, "Tyrone, do you trust me?" "Well, yeah," was the answer I gave. She went on to explain, "If I'm going to fix the problem, you have to give me the remote control." I did, and within minutes she had the machine up and fully operational.

I learned something valuable from that experience. Calling for Andrea's help was good, but not good enough. It wasn't until I released the remote control that I found my answer. Just as I gave the remote to Andrea, we must be willing to give God full control of our lives.

The Lord created us for a successful life. However, this requires learning to lean on Him. And to lean on the Lord means we learn how to accept His help for progress. Now, there is a process to obtaining God's progress and the following account will unfold this very truth.

WE MUST PRAY

Step one to the process is prayer. We need a heart for prayer because this is how we communicate with God. Above all, prayer communicates we need God's help. A man named Jehoshaphat was challenged with a major crisis. Jehoshaphat was the king of Judah and he was helpless until he turned to God.

God's people faced three opposing forces: Moab, Ammon, and a nation from Mount Seir. These enemies desired to dislodge Judah from the land they inherited from the Lord.

Jehoshaphat was notified of the pending danger. And before he allowed fear to dominate the moment, he called a prayer meeting for the entire nation (2 Chron. 20:3–4). This very act delivered a profound declaration to God's people that the Lord was in control.

When you're in need of help, where do you go or who do you call? For the child of God, our help is found in Him. Every crisis will help us discover more about the God we serve. There are no big problems when the Almighty God is concerned. To Him every issue shrinks under His shadow and every predicament yields to His power. He sits high; everyone and everything else is beneath His reign, but not out of His reach.

Jehoshaphat may not have been aware of the strategy of his enemies, but he understood the process to God's progress. Therefore, he prayed to God for help. Now, it's important to differentiate between praying and complaining.

I was taught years ago; if we're going to pray we need not worry, but if we're going to worry we need not pray. Many of God's people spend prayer time telling Him all their problems; they do more listing than listening. Every minute is used worrying as they relay their woes.

Jehoshaphat did not go to God complaining; he prayed. In his prayer he did not consider the bigness of his problem; he meditated on his gargantuan God. When we focus on God's power and not our problems, we talk about His strength not our stress.

Praying to God is not only critical for us, it's important to Him. The Bible records the Lord will silence heaven to hear the prayers of His people (Rev. 8:1–4). God wants to get involved to help us overcome the trials of life, but He will only do it when we invite and invoke His participation through prayer.

WE MUST PROPHESY

The second step in the process is to prophesy. To prophesy means to speak to your circumstances. In other words, when things are going contrary to God's purpose and plan for your life, speak His Word to receive His correction, protection, and direction.

Words are the most powerful tools in the universe. Everything we have and will possess will come by the words we speak. If our words are filled with fear, we'll live defeated; if our words are filled with faith, we'll live victorious (Prov. 18:21).

As Judah anticipated fighting a war against three powerful enemies, they were desperately in need of encouragement. God's people had to be encouraged that victory was possible. They had to know help was not on the way, help was already there.

Victory was proclaimed by one of the servants of God. God's Spirit rested on the priest and he prophesied according to God's plan. The priest told Judah and the inhabitants of Jerusalem not to fear the military forces of their enemies, because the battle belonged to God (2 Chron. 20:15).

God's Word formed the universe and framed the various worlds (Heb. 11:3). And His Word can frame our individual worlds. Just think, our planet is mostly comprised of water and yet it's not flooded. Why? The answer is God's Word prohibits the water from engulfing the earth (Gen. 9:15; Prov. 8:29).

Just as God's Word can withhold the floods, it can prohibit negative influences from overrunning His people. However, having His Word in our hearts is the beginning; we must speak His Word out of our mouths in order to change our negatives to positives. We can either complain how things are going based on what we see, or we can believe and speak God's Word. You see, through prayer we tell God about the problems; through prophecy we tell the problems about our God.

God's Word is the catalyst for change and provides the help we need. In fact, when God sees things are not going according to His divine plan, He speaks in order to make the correction (Rom. 4:17). We must do the same. We can merely talk about what's going wrong, or we can speak by faith and make it right. Therefore, it's vital we learn God's Word and keep it in our hearts in the good times so we can use His Word in the bad times (Luke 6:45). This is exactly what Jehoshaphat and the nation of Judah did.

The priest commanded the people to set themselves, stand still, and see God's Word performed on their behalf. According to the Word of God spoken over their situation, Jehoshaphat and the people were one step closer to their desired progress. However, in order to see their deliverance fully, one final step needed to be performed.

WE MUST PRAISE

Praising God is a sign we already receive the victory. After we have taken our problems to the Lord in prayer and prophesied His Word over our issues, we need to praise God for His provisions.

Before the nation of Judah approached the battlefield to face their foes, they received a word from their king. Jehoshaphat said, "Have faith in the Lord your God, and you will stand strong. Have faith in his prophets, and you will succeed" (2 Chron. 20:20, NCV).

After delivering God's promise of victory, Jehoshaphat appointed a particular group of people to perform the task of singing. This group of people was the tribe of Judah.

The name Judah is derived from the forth son of Jacob. This is important to know because this child was born in difficult times. Leah, the first wife of Jacob, was feeling neglected and didn't receive appreciation from her husband. Leah spent her entire life trying to satisfy Jacob, and her attempts went unrewarded. Finally, when Leah had her fourth child she named him Judah and said, "Now will I praise the LORD" (Gen. 29:35).

In essence, Leah discovered focusing on her problems did her no good; so she decided to focus on her God. Leah is an example for all of God's people today. Many people reserve their praise until they see the odds working in their favor. However, the right kind of praise never waits for the outcome; real praise goes forth in spite of the outcome.

To praise God means to magnify Him. When we magnify the Lord, we express a sincere appreciation for His being in our lives. Those who appreciate God see Him correctly.

How do you see God? Do you see Him as all powerful or just having some power? Do you know the answers to life's enigmas rest in Him? Do you believe He possesses all you need? Even better, are you aware He *is* all you need? When you see God correctly, you'll see the value in His love and receive the help He extends.

It's important to praise the Lord at all times. Whether good or bad; when we're healthy or challenged; through prosperity or seasons of poverty; we must praise the Lord (Ps. 34:1). To praise the Lord in difficult times is an act of our trust in Him. We trust all things eventually work out for our benefit (Rom. 8:28).

When the time for war was upon the nation of Judah, did they sharpen their swords? As they stood before the opposing army, did they spend time counting arrows or strengthening spears? Not at all. Instead of gladiators, Jehoshaphat called for the choir and he commanded them to sing praises to the Lord (2 Chron. 20:21).

As they marched forward singing and giving the Lord high praise, something uncommon occurred. The supernatural intervention of God caused their enemies to attack each other (vv. 22–23). All three armies forgot about their common foe (Judah) and unleashed a bloody assault against one another that left no man standing.

As the people sang praises to the God of the heavens, the Lord sent help to the earth. By the time Jehoshaphat and Judah reached the place of battle, their enemies were totally annihilated. The only thing left for God's people to do was to collect the spoils of their dead rivals. And the treasure was so large it took three days to gather. It was more than they could carry away (vv. 24–25).

Through this account Jehoshaphat and Judah learned the process of progress. They learned this process when facing opposing armies. They discovered God was also known as EL. The name EL is one of many names for God in the Hebrew language.[1] So the next time you're in need of help, if you look close enough you'll discover EL in the midst of h*EL*p.

The Lord revealed the process to progress and His help to me as I struggled giving my wife the remote control to my Blu-ray player. I was willing to ask Andrea for assistance but reluctant to give her the control. It wasn't until I released the control that I was able to enjoy my player.

When we pray to God, prophesy His Word, and give Him the praise He deserves, we'll discover the process to progress. Give God the control to your life; accept His help and discover His enjoyment, excitement, and fulfillment today.

Remember, God will turn your disability into His possibility because He is the *help* for the helpless!

Chapter 2
POINTS TO PONDER

What is the process to receiving God's progress? We must

_____, _____,

and _____.

According to Revelation 8:1–4, what measures does God take to hear your prayers

_____

Have you heard from God lately? If so, what has God revealed to you?

_____

_____

What should you do when you prophesy?

_____

What three things are you to receive from God when you speak His Word?

_____

_____

_____

What are you doing through prayer?

_____

What are you doing through prophecy?

_____

What are you doing when you praise God?

_____

How do you see God?

_____

List some things you can praise God for now:

_____

_____

_____

Those who want to save their lives will give up true life, and those who give up their lives for me will have true life.

—MATTHEW 16:25, NCV

3

Life for the Lifeless
It Takes Three

PURCHASING OUR FIRST home was truly a thrill for Andrea and me. We particularly enjoyed the house-warming gifts we received from family and friends. I'll admit, some of the gifts were impractical but others quite useful; some were extravagant while others were, let's just say— the thought counted.

Of all the gifts we graciously received, the one present I remember the most was a tree. It wasn't a strong oak tree or a full maple tree. To be honest, it was a scrawny twig of a tree, undeveloped and not much to look at. A couple who served with me in the ministry brought the tree over one night and delivered it with much delight.

This was the first house Andrea and I ever purchased, and so we were inexperienced when it came to a lot of things. Being a novice, I asked the couple, "Of all gifts, why a tree?" The wife stepped forward with alacrity and said, "Tyrone, the tree itself is nominal; but the major significance is what the tree represents—life."

After seeing her enthusiasm and hearing her reason, I was both pleased and paused. I was appreciative to receive the tree but apprehensive about my ability to sustain the tree's life.

Noticing my anxiousness, the husband spoke. He reassured me I would do just fine and that owning a tree isn't difficult at all. He told me it took three primary things to ensure the tree's survival—water, soil, and the sun. Armed with that information, I thanked them both and wasted no time in finding the perfect place and planted the tree firmly in my front yard.

Many of God's people are having near-life experiences; meaning they're enduring life, not enjoying life. Living a mundane existence or painfully making it through each day is not the life God intended for us. He wants us to be enlightened, enabled, and encouraged. Thus, we must have the Scriptures, the Spirit, and the Son.

LIFE THROUGH THE SCRIPTURE

God's Scripture enlightens us in the midst of darkness. His Scripture is living, powerful, and proven to provide us with what we need to impact our lives (Heb. 4:12). The Scripture is alive and gives us life (1 Pet. 1:23, NCV). Jesus said, "The words that I speak to you are spirit, and they are life" (John 6:63, NKJV).

A prophet named Ezekiel had a vision in a valley filled with dry bones. Bible scholars have speculated the bones were the remains of soldiers in the Jewish army. These skeletons were scattered, decomposed, and left on the battlefield for scavengers and depraved animals.

Centuries earlier the Lord had given His people His Scripture with a commandment to observe and obey. Their obedience to the Scripture would bring life (Deut. 28:1–2).

However, their neglect would result in their death on the battlefield and their bodies left for the beast to devour (vv. 25–26).

This vision in the valley is not unlike the spiritual condition of many of God's people today. Many people are complaining about having a meaningless life. However, there's no meaning to life without knowing the Giver of life. God gave His Scripture so we may know the truth about Him and accept His life over death.

Unfortunately, we need not look far when it comes to death. Ministries, marriages, and men of all ethnicities are desolate and decaying because they fail to partake of the Scripture.

The Scripture is indicative of water (Eph. 5:26) and is used to irrigate the dryness of our lives. Too many lives are being destroyed due to a lack of appreciation and application of the Scripture. And a dearth of God's Word results in dry lands and barren lives; places where unclean spirits roam and ruin (Luke 11:24–26).

Many of God's people function like desert camels in that they travel far without needing a drink of water. This is not God's design for us. He would rather we imitate the deer which pants for streams of water frequently (Ps. 42:1).

In the valley God enquired if Ezekiel could provide the solution for the dreadful sight. So, the Lord asked, "Can these dry bones live?" (Ezek. 37:3). The stage was set, the revitalization of this dead army hinged upon Ezekiel's answer. Fortunately, the prophet answered correctly. He said, "Lord God, only you know" (Ezek. 37:3, NCV).

The Lord commended him on his answer and told Ezekiel to speak the Scripture over the dry bones (v. 4). God's Scripture brought life in that valley and its potency brings life to the valleys we go through. After we speak God's Scripture to our situations, we must allow His Spirit to have free course.

Life Through the Spirit

The Lord's Spirit enables us to do what we otherwise couldn't and accomplish those things we otherwise wouldn't. In order to have God's power, we need His presence. And that's what His Spirit does; it shows up mightily on our behalf (Acts 2:2). God's Spirit was seen having strength when He answered Job through the whirlwind (Job 38:1) and appeared to Ezekiel through his whirlwind (Ezek. 1:4).

God commanded Ezekiel to speak to the wind (Ezek. 37:9). In this account the natural force of the wind represents the infilling power of God—*His Spirit*. This word *wind* carried the Hebrew concept, *ruah*, and the Greek thought, *pneuma*.

At the creation of the first man, God blew into his nostrils the breath of life. Afterwards man inhaled and exhaled and he became a living soul (Gen. 2:7). The breath man contains in his body is spirit (*ruah*), and as long as he possesses it he lives.

The wind of God being known also as *pneuma* lends itself to the power of God. Thus, God's Spirit enables us to live the life He desires for us. There are those in the family of God who live defeated lives. These same people are settling for less than God's best because they fail to give God's Spirit control and they fail to follow the Spirit's leading.

In life, even if you stumble, you will eventually stand when the Spirit is directing your steps. If you are lacking power, it's because you haven't discovered every predicament you face will be subdued by God's Spirit not your strength (Zech. 4:6).

God carried the prophet Ezekiel by His Spirit and brought him to the valley of dry bones (Ezek. 37:1). Then God ordered the prophet to tell the wind (Spirit) to breathe on the dry bones. So the Spirit obeyed the word of the

Lord and the dry bones awakened, stood on their feet, and became a mighty army (vv. 9–10).

Would you like to resurrect the dead things surrounding your family, finances, and threatening your future? How about breathing fresh life into those issues that appear lifeless? It can happen when you live through the Spirit and look toward the Son.

LIFE THROUGH THE SON

So far we have covered how God grants us life through His Scripture and His Spirit; but what can't be underestimated is the life He gives through His Son.

The Son of God encourages us when we're in despair. Jesus Christ is the Son of God and through Him we are transferred from death to life (John 5:24). In fact, He is life (14:6) and the bringer of bountiful living (10:10).

Ezekiel had the enlightenment of Scripture and the enablement of the Spirit. Now we see him being encouraged by God the Son.

As Ezekiel spoke God's word with authority, something remarkable took place. The bleached bones were covered with flesh, and as skin covered the carcasses they took shape. Silence was replaced by a thundering sound, and the ground quaked beneath the prophet's feet. One by one the shattered skeletons were drawn together and connected to the bone of the Son (Ezek. 37:6–7).

Are you connected to the bones of Jesus? To be connected to His bones means you become so close that you feel what He feels and go where He goes. If you are weary and worn from the pressures of this world, the solution is to connect to Jesus.

Bones that are dry and cracked are missing the marrow of

the Lord. The chronic struggles we face will result in failure. And the stress of life leads to fractures if we don't allow Jesus to live in and through us.

We will never understand God is all we need until He is all we have. Jesus is the chief chiropractor who takes the crooked things in our lives and makes them straight. He's the master surveyor who makes the rough terrain smooth (Isa. 40:4).

Our Lord proclaimed He's the Bread of Life. Many self-proclaimed health gurus argue that bread is not good for us because it's fattening. This notion is conjecture at best. It's true some breads are damaging if consumed in great amounts, but what on earth doesn't hold that effect?

Breads are rich in carbohydrates which are our primary source of energy. Bread also contains dietary fiber. Research has proven a regular intake of fiber keeps our digestive system functioning well and may aid in preventing certain cancers.[1]

Therefore, moderate intake of bread is not fattening; the spreads and fillings we place on bread are the culprits. The same holds true with Jesus. He alone provides the life we need. Therefore, we must move beyond leaning on Jesus *a lot* to leaning on Him *alone*. The Lord does not merely possess what we need, He is all we need. Our concept in life must not be Jesus plus something else; it must be Jesus period— nothing else.

Two of Jesus' followers were walking and discussing the events of Christ's crucifixion. They were heavy of heart and darkened with despair. To them their chances of happiness were dead because their leader was dead.

As Jesus walked with them, He shared from the Scripture and assured them all was happening according to God's divine timetable. The men did not know they were speaking with Jesus until He broke, blessed, and gave them bread

(Luke 24:13–31). When they received the bread, their eyes were opened—no longer seeing His death but now beholding His life. Jesus is the bread that fills the void in our souls.

Having the life of God depends on a confluence of the Scripture, the Spirit, and the Son. The Scripture enlightens us in the dark. The Spirit enables us to avoid defeat. The Son encourages us to trust in the Father's devotion. All three elements play vital roles in our developing into mighty trees in the forest of God.

Well, I did what the couple instructed when they gave Andrea and me a tree as a housewarming gift. I placed the tree in the soil; I provided it with water daily and placed it in the perfect position to receive the sun's rays.

We are no longer living in that house; however, I still drive by just to see my tree. I'm happy to report the tree is enormous. It now overshadows the house. God provides us His Scripture; He places us with His Spirit and positions us to receive His Son. *It takes all three* to provide growth and have life.

Remember, God will turn your disability into His possibility because He is the *life* for the lifeless!

Chapter 3
POINTS TO PONDER

Are you merely enduring life or enjoying life? Explain:

_____

_____

According to the chapter, what three things does God want you to be?

_____

_____

_____

What three things does God give that help you become enlightened, enabled, and encouraged?

_____

_____

_____

How often are you in God's Scripture?

_____

If God's Scripture adds no life to your circumstances, how can you change that?

_____

_____

Salvation gives us the position of a child of God but the Spirit gives us the power of a child of God. Are you lacking power?

_____

How can you allow God's Spirit more access of your life?

_____

_____

You must move beyond leaning on Jesus a lot to leaning on Him _____!

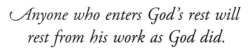

Anyone who enters God's rest will rest from his work as God did.

—HEBREWS 4:10, NCV

4

Rest for the Restless

Let It Hold You

Two shepherds were tending their sheep. While giving their flock water, one of the shepherds accidentally fell in a well. The shepherd in the well began yelling to his partner for help.

The other shepherd immediately lowered one end of a rope down into the deep dark well. He instructed his friend to secure the rope so he could pull him to safety. The shepherd in the well took hold of the rope with a firm grip and hollered to his companion to pull him up.

The shepherd above commenced to pulling his friend out of the well. With each tug of the rope the shepherd being pulled tightened his hold. His knuckles bulged and the skin inside his palms burned from the friction, but still he did his best not to let go of the rope.

The well was deeper than they both imagined and the task of holding the rope became more difficult. Midway up the well the shepherd lost his grip and fell once again. Again, the other shepherd lowered the rope as they repeated the process. Again, the shepherd in the well lost his grip.

Finally, the shepherd outside the well yelled to his partner to try another approach. He instructed him to not hold on to the rope, but rather to tie the rope firmly around his waist. The fallen shepherd did as instructed, and eventually he was pulled to safety.

I know what it's like to fall and need the assistance of someone else and I'm sure you do as well. God is there to help us recover from stumbling and staggering. However, some people are difficult to save because like the shepherd in our opening vignette they're trying to do all the work.

These desperate souls have a tight grip on their finances, a strangle hold on their families, and are grasping at their futures. As they wrestle with life's issues, they are in short supply of rest. They pride themselves on getting things accomplished and starve themselves of peace in the process.

If you stand among the ranks of the weary warriors, tired titans, and all the other fatigued fighters in the world, the Lord is calling you to His rest (Matt. 11:28–30). God truly has rest for the restless.

God's work was documented as finished (Gen. 2:1–3); Jesus' work was declared finished (John 19:30). When Jesus triumphantly uttered the words, "It is finished!" He was finalizing the work of the Father. The term translated, "It is finished," is *tetelestai* in the original Greek language, which means "it is finished, it stands finished, and will always be finished."[3] The work the Lord did can never be undone.

So why are so many followers of God working hard today? Jesus met the demands of God's righteous law. He saw the enormous amount of the bill and paid it in full. Now, instead of God giving us a price, He offers peace; and rather than invoking a rate, we're invited to rest. His peace is for our minds; His rest is for our bodies.

With conviction a parishioner asked his pastor, "What should I do to get saved?" The pastor quickly responded, "You're too late." In fear the parishioner cried, "You mean it's too late to get saved?" "No it's not too late to get saved" replied the pastor, "It's too late to *do* anything, because Jesus did it all."

The key to entering into the rest of the Lord is to believe and receive the finished work of Jesus. The finished work of Jesus encompasses the price He paid, the promise He made, and the prayer He prayed. We don't have to get a hold of the finished work; we just need to allow it to get a hold of us.

Allowing the finished work of Jesus to take hold pulls us out of any negative situation and settles us in the state of God's rest.

THE PRICE JESUS PAID

Jesus paid an awesome price in order to keep us from a terrifying fate. We are all born into sin, we live in sin, and the penalty for our sin is death (Rom. 6:23). Meditate on that! We all were pronounced guilty of the very thing God detests—sin.

Therefore, we all deserved death, but God's judgment was avoided and His wrath averted. When we were headed for an eternity of torment, the flight plans were changed. Did God change how He feels about sin? No, God's sentiments didn't change nor did His sentence, but the candidate did.

We were the candidates for God's punishment, but Jesus exchanged places with us. He went from King to criminal, from the Lawgiver to the lawless, and from identifying with the Father to associating with felons.

Why would Jesus give up so much? Why would He leave deity to slum it with humanity? The answer is unearthed in His Word.

The Bible is God's inspired word to civilization. It is filled with insight and instruction, wisdom and warnings, history and poetry. Every book in the Bible reveals God's will and His ways; they display God's heart and show His hand.

Of all the verses in the Bible, one stands out more than the others. A singular scripture acts as a hinge upon which the others hang—John 3:16. This particular verse uncovers the greatest gift mankind will ever receive—God's love.

John 3:16 stands as the Leaning Tower of Pisa, Taj Mahal, and Buckingham Palace all rolled up in one. It's by far viewed as the Mona Lisa of holy writings. The reason we are left enthralled by this one verse of scripture and captivated with every word is that it delineates God's love.

John 3:16 emphatically declares *who* God loves, "For God so loved the world…" (NKJV). It accurately articulates *how* God loves, "…He gave His only begotten Son…" (NKJV). However, the scripture leaves out *why* God loves. The why is omitted because if there is a "why" it ceases from being love.

Love has no conditions, but it began with the greatest candidate. Love is action and that's exactly what Jesus did for us. When our sin demanded God's divine judgment, Jesus took action. He exhibited His love on the cruelest canvas—the Cross.

Although John 3:16 omitted the "why," it does conclude with a *what*. It tells us what it takes to receive God's pardon from punishment: "…whoever believes in Him should not perish but have everlasting life" (NKJV). To believe in Jesus opens and ushers in God's rest. We can rest knowing *the breadth of God's love reaches everyone and the depth of God's love was the giving of His Son.*

The price Jesus paid was great, but He paid it gladly because

His love for us is greater (Heb. 12:2). (We'll discuss more on God's love in chapter 12.)

THE PROMISE JESUS MADE

Jesus made a promise to all who follow Him. He promised to prepare and reserve a place for us (John 14:2). The purpose of His promise was to put us at rest. Allow me to share an experience I believe expresses the promise Jesus made.

My wife and I decided to take our daughters and spend the Fourth of July weekend in San Antonio, Texas. We were visiting our son Omarr, who had joined a spiritual enrichment center.

The evening before our departure I reserved a room in a grand hotel. At the time my daughters were still fairly young, so I reserved a room large enough to accommodate four people. The hotel was situated right on the River Walk, so this was ideal and convenient for shoppers like my wife.

On the morning of our trip before we took to the road, I led my family in a short prayer. We asked God for His protection, guidance, provision, and above all—His favor. I concluded the prayer by mentioning a verse from the Bible (Eph. 3:20).

When we connected with our son in San Antonio, he expressed his desire to spend the weekend with us at the hotel. Since it was Fourth of July weekend, the hotel lobby was bustling with guests. We stood in a check-in line resembling the lines formed at Walmart during Black Friday.

Once we reached the front desk, we were greeted and served by the hotel's head clerk. I requested an additional room now that Omarr was joining us. I was not surprised when the clerk announced the hotel was full to capacity. Before I could express any disappointment, the clerk looked into his monitor and saw something that turned the predicament in our favor.

The head clerk remarked, "Mr. Holcomb, I see you are a gold card member and a loyal guest." Honestly, I didn't recall having such status, but I smiled and quickly agreed. To my surprise the head clerk declared, "We do have one suite available—the presidential suite." Even more amazing, he said, "I'm giving you the presidential suite for no additional charge." We received a $1,600 per night suite for only $298.

After we were given the keys to the suite, I thanked him for his gesture, which to us was largesse. As we were getting on the elevator, one of the bellhops commented, "You're getting the best room in the hotel; make sure you take care of it."

After hearing his remarks, Andrea was upset and wanted to give the bellhop a few choice words of her own. I instructed Andrea to ignore his remark. I reminded her that we were on our way up and to not allow anyone to bring her attitude down. We serve the only wise God, and the devil was reduced to making wisecracks.

My friend, the Lord, has declared us gold card members in His family. Our status is declared in His Word (1 Pet. 2:9). Our position is set; our place is sure. Jesus said we will be with Him (John 14:3); the promise of spending eternity in His presence is overwhelming to me.

Don't allow anyone to rain on your parade or bring you down; your place is up. Rest knowing the Lord has a place for you; and since God said it that settles it.

The Prayer Jesus Prayed

When many people think of Jesus praying, the Book of Luke chapter 11 comes to mind. This is where we'll find what's considered the Lord's Prayer, but this was actually a model prayer Jesus taught His disciples.

We find what Jesus prayed for all His followers in the Book of John chapter 17. In His prayer Jesus asked God the Father to allow us to share His life (vv. 1–5), know His name (vv. 6–12), have His Word (vv. 13–19) and see His glory (vv. 20–26). And ensconced in His many requests, Jesus prayed to the Father to keep us from evil (v. 15).

It doesn't matter what trouble we face, we have the heavenly host watching out for us. We can take comfort in knowing we're never overlooked; we always have the Father looking over us. His thoughts of us are of peace and not evil and He will bring us to good fortune (Jer. 29:11).

Jesus prayed to the Father to keep us (John 17:11); this reveals His value for us. Anything of no value can be lost and forgotten, but those things of great worth must be kept someplace secure. God the Father created us, He placed within us great treasure (2 Cor. 4:7), and He keeps an eye on His investment.

God assures us of His ever presence because we're valuable to Him. The world brings its temptations, tests, and trials; but God's presence affords us provision, protection, and power. Jesus said we can overcome this world's tribulations when we understand He has gone before us and toppled anything that stands in our way, and He also noted our peace is found in Him (John 16:33). To secure the peace we need there must be a total acceptance of the finished work of Christ.

The shepherd who fell in the well thought he could climb out by his own strength. When he was given a rope he grabbed and pulled instead of wrapping himself and resting in it.

After several attempts he decided to take the advice and assistance of his friend. He stopped his feeble attempts of holding onto the rope and allowed the rope to hold him. Therefore, when he rested he was rescued.

God does not want us in the pit of life; He desires our freedom from the dark as we walk in the light of liberty. This happens when we allow our minds to be wrapped in the finished work of Jesus.

Jesus paid the price, made the promise, and prayed the prayer. *He did it!* So in everything—let it hold you.

Remember, God will turn your disability into His possibility because; He is the *rest* for the restless!

Chapter 4
POINTS TO PONDER

According to the chapter, Jesus' work is finished. What does this mean to you?

_____

_____

The key to entering the Lord's rest involves what two things?

_____ and

_____ the Lord's finished work.

John 3:16 declares what two things about God's love?

_____

_____

John 3:16 omits something important concerning God's love. What is it?

_____

Are you able to find rest in the Lord's promises? Is there a particular promise you're resting in now? If so, record it here:

_____

_____

Are you aware God esteems and sees great value in you? Take the time and find scriptures that reveal your worth to God and write them:

_____

According to the chapter we receive three things as a result of God's presence. What are these three things?

_____

_____

_____

*All who make themselves clean from
evil will be used for special purposes.
They will be made holy, useful to the
Master, ready to do any good work.*

—2 Timothy 2:21, ncv

5

Use for the Useless
No Excuses

THE AFTERNOON SPARKED with enthusiasm as commuters and pedestrians filled the streets with excitement. The shopping district's heart beat with the rhythm of purpose. As the sun smiled you could feel the wind's soft pleasing whisper.

Everyone scurried about; some were shopping, others taking a lunch break; all of them vibrant and busy. Each person was full of activity with the exception of one—the invisible man.

His body collapsed on the ground, his posture motionless. His clothes were tattered and soiled. His figure was masked with fatigue and filth. The only possession he claimed was a bucket. He was an oxymoron, a dead man breathing. He readily welcomed looks of disappointment or disdain because it would have meant they were looking. Instead, he had to settle for indifference.

Day after day he appeared as a smudge on the city's canvas. Never was he seen as a man, but rather a mistake. Until it happened! A fairly young man approached him and did the unthinkable—spoke. His voice was warm and inviting as he asked the vagabond these simple words, "May I use your bucket?"

Stunned, the vagrant could only respond, "You want to use my bucket?" "Yes, may I use your bucket?" the young man repeated. The homeless man acquiesced and gave his only possession.

Like the vagrant, many of God's people feel useless. Somewhere on life's journey failures and faults led to disappointment and disconnection. They have pulled away from society and have settled for a life of insignificance.

At one point they set sail to explore vast opportunities only to become shipwrecked on the sea of obscurity. For these people eager anticipation for success has been replaced with fractured dreams and fragmented pieces of hope.

Now I say to the discarded, disqualified, discouraged, and disgruntled; all is not lost because you're not lost. The Lord sees directly where you are. Society may consider you a castaway, downcast, or outcast; but God has made you a part of His cast.

In our society there are three groups of people who, for the most part, are deemed useless—the *too young*, *too old*, and the *handicapped*. Anyone of these categories could render a person useless, given certain conditions. However, each of these categories is deemed efficient and effective to God.

God Can Use the Too Young

The Lord's power extends beyond the boundaries we set. He can accomplish victory for us at any level. However, some are disqualified by others because they're considered too young for the task. Yet, youthfulness can become a resourceful commodity in the hands of a mighty God. The following account will allude to this very fact.

There he stood enormous and solid as steel. As his frame stretched to the heavens, his voice thundered threats which brought soldiers to their knees. His name was Goliath, and he was the legendary champion of the Philistines (1 Sam. 17).

Goliath was a tower of intimidation with power equaling a regiment. And this mammoth of a man challenged the entire Jewish army and shook his fist at the living God. As a battering-ram for the devil, Goliath was preparing to smash any challenger.

The king of Israel searched his forces for a man to defeat this foe. Nevertheless, his search was unfruitful, for every man cringed at the idea of standing before the terrible titan. Attempting to arouse courage within the ranks, the king offered a reward to any man who would face off with the giant. And still there were no takers; none except one—David.

Young David was delivering food to his older brothers when he happened to hear Goliath spewing one insult after another toward God's people. Once David heard the challenges of the gladiator, he volunteered to cut Goliath down to size.

At first no one took David's offer seriously—not his brothers, not the king, and certainly not Goliath—because David was too young. David's small body was not fit for soldier's armor and his hands were not accustomed to handling a sword. Even still, there David stood—too small, too naïve, too young.

The king felt he had no choice and David had no chance, but he allowed the young man to enter combat. This was a battle of epic proportions, but it was perceived as a fight between a grizzly and a gazelle. Everyone favored Goliath to win except David, who placed his faith in God.

When the dust settled the young David stood with a

slingshot in one hand and the giant's head in the other. Before anyone could realize what had happened, David was delivering his celebratory speech.

When facing opposition, God can make the too young too strong. He is able to do for us what we are unable to do for ourselves. God defies reason and His ways are beyond our finite imaginations. And, just as God can mature the young, He is able to rejuvenate the old.

GOD CAN USE THE TOO OLD

While some people feel useless because they're too young, others feel the bite of inadequacy because they're too old. These people feel their best years are in the rearview mirror, but such a perception is far from the truth.

God can use anyone who is willing to yield to His authority. There is no such thing as too old for God; after all He is the Ancient of Days. God can make the aging ageless for His glory. To amplify this point let's consider a man named Caleb (Num. 13–14; Josh. 14–15).

This man served Moses without inhibitions. He was part of the generation that made the great Diaspora from Egypt to the Promised Land. Many of God's people found reason to complain and discourage Moses, but Caleb was not named among them. The Bible records that Caleb followed Moses fully because of his faith in the living God (Num. 32:11–12).

Caleb was given the promise to receive land for him and his family at the age of forty. He was faithful to his leader and, more importantly, to his God throughout his life. By faith he endured many battles. This man witnessed numerous changes during his lifetime; the landscapes changed, the leaders changed, and his body changed. He evolved from an adolescent to an adult to the elderly.

Although Caleb's body grew old, his spirit remained new (2 Cor. 4:16). His renewed spirit allowed him to endure; and at the age of eighty-five he was able to see God's promise fulfilled. God allows us to endure tests, trouble and even time. Forty-five years after receiving God's promise, Caleb was able to boldly declare and claim what was rightfully his (Jos. 14:11–12). Caleb did not consider his aging body; he placed his confidence in his faithful God.

My friend, with God you're never outdated, old-fashioned, or out of time. Has God made you a promise? Look to Him to perform it and don't consider your strength, meditate on His. Too old is not a part of God's vocabulary. He doesn't place His people out to pasture or release them to retirement. With God the command is not retire, it's re-fire.

God Can Use the Handicapped

God can turn our disabilities to possibilities. No one needs to hear that more than the handicapped. The Lord will take the handicapped and make them handy. He is the source for those who lack resources; the sun ray for those in darkness; the repairer of broken lives. The following account reveals this perfectly.

Mephibosheth was the son of a prince, grandson to King Saul. His grandfather was the first king of Israel and their family was revered throughout the regions. Born into royalty Mephibosheth was set to have the finest commodities and to live the life of luxury. However, this was not his story (2 Sam. 4:4; 9).

Unfortunately, Mephibosheth's father, Jonathan, was killed in battle when he was only five years old. His grandfather Saul took his own life to avoid being captured by the Philistines. Fearing young Mephibosheth's life was also in danger, his caretaker fled with him. In her haste she dropped Mephibosheth and crippled him in both feet.

Taken from his home, Mephibosheth spent his developing years in a place called Lo-Debar, which in the Hebrew language meant "no word." In essence, the life of the prince remained on pause; he had no communication. Then one day God placed it on King David's heart to bless someone from King Saul's lineage for the sake of his friend Jonathan.

Now an adult Mephibosheth was taken to meet King David. In his crippled state, Mephibosheth fell to the ground and bowed before the king. David told him not to fear and that he would restore his estate. David also made a place for Mephibosheth at the royal dining table.

To all these blessings Mephibosheth replied, "Who am I that you would look at a dead dog like me?" The sad commentary is Mephibosheth viewed himself as useless. When the time called for rejoicing, he mourned; when the king pointed to blessings, Mephibosheth pointed out his burdens.

Fortunately, Mephibosheth's handicap did not stop the blessings of God. He was given land with a host of servants to provide for his needs. Also, he spent the rest of his days eating at the king's table as one of David's sons.

My friend, maybe you are in a place of Lo-Debar where there is no communication. If you feel someone has dropped you and crippled your chances of happiness, consider this: God's plan for your life is not over (Jer. 29:11). This is what the vagrant in our opening story discovered.

Stunned at the request, the homeless man allowed the stranger to use his bucket. The young man positioned himself down next to the disheveled man and began using the bucket as a drum. Every beat of the bucket created a rhythm that resonated in the beggar's heart. When the young man ceased the beggar whispered his approval.

Then the young man said, "Let's go again, but this time we'll add this…" The young man removed his hat and placed it right side up on the ground. Again, he played the bucket with precision and caused passersby to pause. One by one people started placing money into the hat. Then another man emerged from the onlookers with an acoustic guitar.

This man positioned himself down on the other side of the homeless man and strummed his guitar adding the perfect complement to the bucket's beats. Finally, a young lady came forth from the crowd. As she squatted beside the musical ensemble she provided harmonious vocals that left the gatherers in awe.

When the impromptu concert was complete, the trio and the vagrant received adulation and applause. Each member thanked the other for joining in the session. They looked to the homeless man and returned his bucket along with a hat filled with money.

As the audience dispersed and the musical trio disappeared, tears were the outward sign of the inward joy felt by the wearied traveler. This man thought his bucket useless and discovered it was a resource to bring prosperity.

God desires to take what others consider useless and make use of it. Remember this: *Without God, we cannot; however, without us, God will not.* The Lord wants us to allow Him to make the kind of music with our lives that will bring joy to others.

Give the bucket with no excuses. Whether too young, too old, handicapped, or otherwise, God makes use of the useless.

Remember, God will turn your disability into His possibility because He is the *use* for the useless!

Chapter 5
Points to Ponder

Do you feel useless or important? Explain:

_____

_____

What has God done for you that you were unable to do for yourself?

_____

_____

Your best years are not behind you, they are before you. Write your future plans:

_____

_____

_____

_____

Do you have an attribute you considered useless but after reading this chapter you've discovered it can be used to bring success? Please write it:

_____

_____

_____

_____

*Our God… We don't know what
to do, so we look to you for help.*

—2 CHRONICLES 20:12, NCV

6

Clue for the Clueless
Never Mind How; Look at Who

J OHN AND HIS wife were doing fairly well. He had received his doctorate degree from Columbia University. They had bought a home and were ready to have children. John was satisfied with his career choice and had considered starting his own business. By all accounts everything seemed well and the future looked promising for this young couple—until the unthinkable occurred.

During the regular course of his day, John began feeling fatigued. An average exercise like walking became difficult as he would experience pain in his joints. At first John didn't think anything was serious. He attributed his tiredness and joint pain to an overactive lifestyle.

However, the complications intensified enough to warrant a visit to his family physician. John's doctor assessed his symptoms and decided he needed a blood test. He informed John that he would receive a call when the lab results were confirmed.

A week later, John received a call from the clinic. His second visit with his physician was devastating. The doctor informed John that his test results revealed he had leukemia. He further explained John would have to undergo chemotherapy and a bone marrow transplant. Finally, the doctor stressed a need for a donor.

Crushed beneath the weight of this diagnosis, John's mind filled with questions. How was he going to tell his wife the heart wrenching news? How long would the treatment take and would it even work? How difficult would it be to identify a perfect match for the bone marrow transplant? How would this disease affect his lifestyle?

How? This simple question packs an enormous punch. It's the initial question on the path of uncertainty. We ask, "How?" when we are searching for solutions to problems that bombard our reality. The question, "How?" is a knee-jerk inquiry when we're in short supply; it's the panic button we push in the midst of a crisis. Even when we don't ask, "How?" outwardly, the question lingers inwardly.

The Bible records the tragedy of a man named Job. This man had a reverence for God and repugnance for evil. He was on the Lord's honor roll when it came to character and conduct (Job 1:8). Job was wealthy and held the distinguished honor of being the greatest man in his sector (v. 3). However, having prestige, prosperity, and power didn't prevent Job's world from shattering.

This man had to determine how to get from catastrophe to harmony, how to remain calm in calamity, and how to reassemble the pieces to his scattered life. All at once he needed to know how to fix his finances, his family, and his frailties.

As we explore his trials, I'm certain we'll uncover answers for our own. Let's discover what to do when we don't have a clue.

How to Fix Our Finances

Job was a man of great means and his estate extended from livestock to fruit bearing lands. He possessed seven thousand sheep, three thousand camels, and five hundred donkeys just for starters (Job 1:3).

I imagine his house aesthetically replete with precious stones and fine art. His furniture was probably created from the finest materials imported from distant lands. The crowning jewel of his mansion may have been his bathhouse that came equipped with cascades and private villas.

Then tragedy struck! In one day Job went from having it all to staring at nothing. He moved from Royalty Boulevard to Penury Lane faster than you can say jumping jack flash. Job digressed from beholding a fat bank account to bemusing a big fat "how." How did his fortune turn so quickly?

Have you ever ridden the financial roller-coaster? Has your economic situation turned from positive to negative so fast you almost got whiplash? If so, you understand the plight of Job.

In these troublesome times how do we keep our eyes on the Lord and not the stock market? We do so with an understanding that God is our source and everything else is a resource. The Lord is able to sustain us in our lack and bring His abundance before us.

Sadly, many of God's people are under a misconception about money. These people either have the wrong perception about prosperity or they see no purpose for it. The wrong perception of prosperity leads us to believe God gives us money just so we can spend it on a life of luxury and leisure. However, if we contend that money serves no purpose and has no place for those who follow Christ, we are sadly mistaken.

The Bible teaches two primary reasons why God wants us

wealthy. The first reason is so we may establish His covenant here on earth and are able to give toward every good work (Deut. 8:18; 2 Cor. 9:8). The second reason is so we may have resources to give to those who are in need (Eph. 4:28).

This is exactly what Job was noted for; he instructed and strengthened many people (Job 4:3–4). He also provided financial means for those who were in need (29:12–13, 15–16). When we learn to seek God's prosperity for the right reasons, He will fix our finances.

Let not selfish pursuits dominate our thoughts but allow God's plan for the advancement of His kingdom to take precedent. Does this mean we can't enjoy life's creature comforts? Of course we can, God wants us to enjoy life's amenities. However, it's when we pursue His presence, plan, and purpose that He adds life's necessities and pleasures (Matt. 6:33).

God took Israel to a place flowing with milk and honey (Exod. 3:8), and He is still leading His people to milk and honey today. Milk represents our necessities and honey is symbolic of our luxuries.

When it comes to our finances, we must have the resolve of Job; it was the Lord who gave it, so if He takes it away we will still bless His name (Job 1:21–22). Job's declaration of blessing shows he valued his God more than his finances. When your financial test comes will you value God also?

How to Fix Our Family

Job was blessed by God with seven sons and three daughters (Job 1:2). It would have been great if his children had emulated their father's faithfulness to the Lord. However, this appears not to have been the case. While Job spent time praying and fasting, his children were playing and feasting. Job prayed continuously for his children's spiritual condition, but saw no improvement (v. 5).

Just when Job thought matters couldn't get worse, they did. His children went from being spiritually dead to physically dead.

One evening the siblings gathered at the oldest brother's home. As they spent the evening eating and drinking wine a strong wind struck the house. The roof collapsed crushing the children in the process (vv. 18–19).

In one moment Job's family was reduced drastically. With his children gone Job and his wife were left examining the carnage. Can you imagine a funeral with ten caskets?

I'm sure this couple experienced pain on a colossal level. However, rather than drawing closer to each other, their agony pushed them apart. On one occasion, tempers flared and tension was at an all-time high. Job's wife told him to curse God and die. Job's reply was just as sharp, he compared her to a foolish woman (2:9–10).

Although Job argued with his wife, he never allowed their disagreement to turn his affections from her. This man made a promise to himself to be faithful to his wife (31:1, 9–10); and I believe his covenant kept them through the turbulence.

Unfortunately, in ministry I have witnessed the dismantling of too many families. I have seen my share of couples contaminating their union with selfishness. And the number of fractured families is increasing daily.

The question becomes, "How do we fix our families?" The answer is not in self-help books or on daytime talk shows; the answer to the family struggles is God. He gives us grace for our grief, peace for our problems, and wisdom for our worries.

When tragedy struck Job's family, he immediately fell down and worshipped God (1:20). When tragedy hits our household, we should do the same. However, many of God's people abandon Him in disappointment. Remember, *a disappointment to us is only an appointment with God.* Nothing takes Him by surprise.

If your family becomes torn apart, know God specializes in sewing. He's the maker of our lives and the mender of our hearts. He has a blueprint for broken homes and holds the pattern for scattered pieces. Trust Him to do what you're unable to do and see your family together and strong.

How to Fix Our Frailties

The devil uses copious tactics to distract and destroy our faith in God. Satan took Job's finances, yet Job remained faithful. He attacked Job's family; however, Job blessed the Lord. As a final attempt the devil made Job frail.

The devil accused Job of not caring enough about his finances and family. He argued the case of self-preservation by saying Job would break under the pressure of sickness (Job 2:4–5).

Job found himself in the furnace of affliction; it seemed his sufferings were multiplying by the moment. He developed painful sores from his head to his feet (v. 7).

Out of the frying pan into the fire was a term Job became acquainted with first hand. He had lost all he owned. The only thing that outweighed his personal loss was the excruciating pain that engulfed his body. Mentally—he went from harmony to agony. Emotionally—he went from wow to woe. Physically—he went from super to suffering.

Job's life was reduced to rubbish, and his sickness added insult to injury. He positioned himself in the ashes of his possessions and with a piece of pottery he scrapped the sores on his body (v. 8).

It appeared sickness had taken its toll; Job cursed the day he was born (3:1–3). In his frailness Job had questions for God. Do you blame him? I too have wondered where God was when illness attacked my body and how I would recover. Remember John? When leukemia took a hold of his body, he wondered how as well.

As his condition unraveled, John contemplated how to break the news to family. How long would he need treatment? How would the disease affect his lifestyle? How successful would the bone marrow transplant be? The pervasive question that echoed was, How? How?? How???

Have you ever asked how? If so, you stand with the majority not the minority. The question of "How?" bombards the minds of many of God's people. How can we fix our finances? How can we fix our families? How can we fix our frailties? We fix them with our faith in the living God.

Job vacillated in his emotions as he questioned God; but when God finally spoke up, it was Job who had to answer up. God redirected Job's focus from *how* to *Who*!

The Lord told Job to gather himself and stand like a man. Afterwards, the Lord hit Job with questions of His own. However, God's questions were not on *how*; He fired off a series of *who* (Job 38:5–6, 8, 25, 29, 36–37, 41; 39:5).

We must never mind (give attention to) how but look at *who*. In essence, we must not waste time wondering *how* we will be delivered; we must focus our attention on *who* delivers. Many are the afflictions of the righteous, but the Lord delivers us from them all (Ps. 34:19). The difference between the words *how* and *who* is in the way the letters are arranged. God wants us to know as we rearrange the letters; He will rearrange our lives.

Once Job focused totally on God, he placed his hand over

his mouth (Job 40:3–5). Job admitted before his trials he had only heard of God, but through his trials he had seen the Lord for himself (42:5). He rearranged his *how* to his *who* and received double for his trouble (vv. 12–17).

As for John, he took his focus off the diagnosis and his donor and started trusting the skill of his doctor. His leukemia was successfully treated and God has added children to their union. Like John, we need not consider the diagnosis of our problems; we must have faith in Jesus the Great Physician.

We must keep our faith in God intact especially when we're under attack. We are not to live off His explanations; we are to live on His promises.

Remember, God will turn your disability into His possibility because; He is the *clue* for the clueless!

Chapter 6
POINTS TO PONDER

According to the chapter, what are the two primary reasons God wants us wealthy.

_____

_____

Spiritually speaking, what does God's milk represent?

_____

Spiritually speaking, what does God's honey represent?

_____

Do you currently have family issues that need God's attention? If so, write what you need God to do.

_____

_____

_____

Are you currently trying to figure out "how" a matter can be fixed? If so, focus on "*who*" fixes all matters. Write down all the different attributes of Jesus from the Book of John.

_____

_____

_____

_____

_____

The LORD says, "I will make you wise and show you where to go. I will guide you and watch over you."

—PSALM 32:8, NCV

7

Aim for the Aimless
God Knows the Way

I RECALL THE FIRST fully loaded vehicle I owned. The car was the perfect color equipped with many instruments and controls such as an automatic moon-roof, heated seats and steering wheel, Bose audio system, XM satellite radio, Bluetooth hands free phone system and the list goes on. Of all the features my car provided the one I came to appreciate the most was the navigation system.

Now, unlike my wife, I'm not eager to learn new devices. Andrea reads a learner's manual like Sherlock Holmes reads clues. As for me, I read manuals like a five-year-old with a text book on Western Philosophy (I couldn't care less). So you can imagine what happened when I got in my car, turned on my navigation system and saw the guidance menu glowing—dare I say deer in headlights.

The menu listed the following categories: map settings, setting destination, route guidance, storing locations, voice recognition and more. Overwhelmed, I decided to forego the experience altogether. After all, I knew my way around the city pretty well and didn't need a GPS (Global Positioning System) getting in the way.

I owned my car for over a year when Andrea and I decided to visit a theater for the purpose of seeing a play. The play was in Dallas, Texas and we had never been to that particular venue. Andrea was excited about the trip and so was I with the exception of one thing—I had to use my GPS.

As I activated the system a look of bewilderment covered my face. My confusion turned to frustration and before full-blown agitation took over, Andrea said, "Tyrone, this is easy." She went on to say the navigation system had voice command. Andrea took me through the voice recognition procedure, inputted our destination and we were on the way.

There comes a time in everyone's life when direction is needed. Some people need to know who to marry; which career to pursue or college to attend. These are only a few examples of life's puzzles that need figuring out.

No matter what situation we face we must learn to seek God for the solution. The Lord sees the difficulties that we encounter and He wants to come to our aid, but we must trust Him. As we trust God, He will navigate us through the obstacles that are prohibiting us from moving forward.

Trusting God is the essential theme in the Book of Exodus. The Lord made His presence known to Moses and revealed His desire to rescue Israel (Exod. 3:7–8, 10). However, their deliverance from persecution and bondage would rely on their ability to follow the Lord's direction.

COME OUT OF THE WORLD

Israel moved to Egypt in search of a better life and received what they anticipated. They were given fine clothing, food in abundance and the best land to tend their flocks. They had great possessions, grew strong and their families multiplied in numbers (Gen. 47:27). All was well in Egypt until a despot took authority and proclaimed Israel enemies of state (Exod. 1:8–10).

Israel had come to depend on the resources of Egypt and the good graces of the Pharaoh. However, times had changed and so did the feelings of the Egyptians towards God's people. Israel was no longer treated as welcomed guest, but rather forced into a life of slavery.

Israel was subjugated and forced into hard labor. These shepherds were made to build with brick and mortar, work countless hours in the fields and accept ruthless treatment from their oppressors (Exod. 1:14). Israel's future predicted only pain and persecution, but God remembered His promise (Gen. 15:12–14).

After 400 years of bondage and burden the Lord called a man named Moses to carry His message of deliverance. Moses was instructed to take this message to the Pharaoh of Egypt and more importantly to the people of God.

Before accepting his assignment Moses conveyed his own inadequacy. Moses admitted he was short-handed; God revealed His far reach. Moses fumbled over how to perform the task; God caused him to focus on Who would perform the task (Exod. 3:14). In essence, God was the True Deliverer; Moses just needed to follow directions.

Where are you right now? Are you grappling with a decision or contemplating which direction? Have you become so dependent on the world that your life is filled with fear? If you have become burdensome God has heard your cry and has dispatched your deliverance.

Allow the Lord to be your navigation system. He can direct you through traffic and aim you toward your destination. In times of trouble, God says, "Go right." In areas where there are obstacles, He commands, "Go around." Those places that are undeveloped, He directs us to "Go through."

So, in order for God to deliver His people from bondage He had to reveal His omnipotence to the Egyptians. God performed ten miracles in the sight of Pharaoh and each miracle was a direct challenge to the foreign gods. Through every plague the Lord's power was displayed while Pharaoh was proven powerless.

Eventually the Pharaoh capitulated and released his tight grip from Israel. God's people were liberated and compensated for years of mistreatment (Exod. 12:32–36).

In the Bible, Egypt typifies the world. The Lord delivered Israel from Egypt then, and He'll deliver us from the world now. God plans a way for us to escape the world's influence, but that's only the beginning. After we come out of the world we must go through the wilderness.

Go Through the Wilderness

Unfortunately, too many of God's people have come out of the world, but are stuck in the wilderness. In Egypt God showed Israel His ability to protect; in the wilderness He displayed His knack to provide.

In the wilderness Israel complained continuously concerning their welfare. They witnessed God's ability to free them from their aggressors, but doubted His competence to sustain them on their journey. Their wondering brought about their wandering. Instead of going through the wilderness, they traveled around in the wilderness.

The Lord wanted to extend His blessings, after they had learned His lessons. From Egypt He brought them; in the wilderness He taught them. The lesson God desired to teach was the importance of trust. Israel had to learn to trust the Lord in every area and at every turn.

Israel entered the classroom of God and witnessed Him open the Red Sea for them and close it on their pursuers (Exod. 14:21–30). They observed the Lord make the bitter waters of Marah sweet to drink (Exod. 15:23–25). They experienced the Lord's graciousness as He provided manna for their hunger (Exod. 16:11–18). The Lord did these miracles and more to prove His provisions.

Every child of God can evaluate whether they're in the wilderness. The determining factor for going through or staying in the wilderness is being *compliant* or having a *complaint*. Being compliant means we obey the Lord's direction; having a complaint means we object to the Lord's leading.

The difference in the spelling of compliant and complaint is where the letter "i" is placed. Thus, the revelation here is on where we place our "eye." Do you look around aimlessly or look up to God and receive aim?

It's paramount to learn Who God is in order for us to go through wilderness experiences. Therefore, God declares to the philosopher, He's The Truth; to the astrologists, He's The Bright and Morning Star. The Lord reveals to the geologists, He's The Rock of all ages; to the gardener, He's The Lily of the valleys. God beckons to the baker, He's The Bread of Life; to the jeweler, He's The Pearl of great price. The Lord announces to the sick, He's The Great Physician; and to the lost, He's the Way. Discover for yourself the many facets of the Lord.

There's no need to wonder or wander in the wilderness; just believe and receive God knows the way, because He is the Way.

STAY IN THE WAY

The only method of going through the wilderness successfully is to go God's way. Jesus is the Way of God! (John 14:6). Since Jesus is the Way, *we must see Him **on** our way and not **in** the way.* We are to lean on the Lord and in all our ways acknowledge Him and submit to His direction (Prov. 3:5–6). Once we know Jesus is the Way our trust must remain in Him.

After years of wandering in the wilderness, Israel finally arrived at the border of their Promised Land. However, they did not learn to trust God's Word completely. Instead of entering in and claiming their possession, they asked Moses to send in spies to survey the area.

Moses brought their request before God and the Lord allowed them to do it their way. God permitted their petition not because their way was better; He wanted them to discover His promises could only be obtained His way.

Moses sent twelve spies to scour the land. When the scouts returned they had conflicting reports. Ten spies complained about the inhabitants of the land. They told tales of monster sized menaces who could crush God's people like grasshoppers. They also spoke of land which devoured its inhabitants (Num. 13:32–33). Even still, there were two spies who reported the land just as God promised. One of the two named Caleb announced, "Let us go up at once, and possess it; for we are well able to overcome it" (Num. 13:30).

When the people of God heard the conflicting reports they had a choice to respond in fear or in faith. They chose fear and denied the way of the Lord. The people rose up against their leaders and made plans to return to Egypt (Num. 14:4). For their insolence and disobedience, the Lord was set to destroy them. However, due to the pleading of Moses, God spared their lives, but prohibited all but the two believing spies from receiving the promise (Num. 14:11–23).

My friend, let's not be like that unbelieving generation who was delivered from the world, brought through the wilderness, but failed in the way. Understand, the will of God is promised; the grace of God is provided and the way of God is proven. All we need is faith in God (Mark 11:22).

When your family appears to be falling apart; have faith in God. When your finances are low; have faith in God. When the job market is scarce or you're under qualified; have faith in God. Stop wondering how God is going to help because wondering eventually leads to wandering. Don't try to figure out what only God can work out. Let Him navigate your path because His way is pleasant (Ps. 23:2).

On our way to Dallas Andrea and I encountered road construction, alternate routes and heavy traffic. All these distractions had me on edge because I didn't want to be late or miss the play altogether.

I'll admit a couple of times I tried to take a way that seemed familiar and every time I ran into detours. Finally, Andrea convinced me to trust the navigation system. She told me to allow the GPS to do what it was designed to do—show us the way. I submitted, followed the GPS and we arrived on time and enjoyed the play immensely.

You know, after some years passed, Israel learned to trust their GPS (God's Positioning System). As a result of their trust, they enjoyed their Promised Land.

Through faith and obedience, let Him bring you out of the world, take you through the wilderness, as you go His way.

Remember, God will turn your disability into His possibility because; He is the *aim* for the aimless!

Chapter 7
POINTS TO PONDER

Are you grappling with a decision or contemplating which direction to take? If so, explain:

_____

_____

The world's web can hold us in bondage and fear. Is there anything holding you that you need to give God power over? If so, explain:

_____

_____

According to the chapter, explain the difference between being compliant and making a complaint.

_____

_____

According to the chapter who is the Way of God?

_____

According to the chapter, the will of God is _____, the grace of God is _____ and the way of God is _____.

Write the steps you can take to stay in God's Way.

_____

_____

So Jesus went with the men. He was getting near the officer's house when the officer sent friends to say, "Lord, don't trouble yourself, because I am not worthy to have you come into my house."

—LUKE 7:6, NCV

8

Worth for the Worthless
Who He Is; I Am His

APRIL 23, 1985, has been noted as a day of commercial catastrophe. Before this day the Coca Cola Company was considered the soft drink giant. However, the company made a decision that would serve as a warning for the world of marketing.[1]

After having ninety-nine successful years of serving their consumer's favorite formula, the company decided to make a change. The Coca Cola brand began feeling the heat of competition from their leading competitors. Even though the Cola industry as a whole was in a slump, the Coca Cola Company saw declining product sales for fifteen consecutive years.

In an attempt to boost sales, the chief executives at the company decided to shake things up a bit by changing the age old formula. In the summer of 1985, the company introduced their new formula and renamed their product "New Coke." Well, they certainly shook things up; but much to their chagrin, the market went into shock.

Consumers all over the nation released an outcry of utter

displeasure. The company had a phone line that was inundated with consumer complaints. In fact, all the Coca Cola offices around the country received calls from disgruntled customers. Calls spiked from 400 to 1,500 per day.[2]

Protests groups arose to "bring back the 'old' Coke."[3] Protesters begin picketing Coca Cola events with signs that read, "We want the real thing"![4] Many in the marketing world considered the events that took place in the summer of '85 the "marketing blunder of the century."[5] It became quite clear to the chief executives that returning to Coca Cola's original formula was their only viable option.

What would make a highly successful conglomerate like Coca Cola alter their famed formula? For that matter, what would make a tenured professor consider switching universities or faithful spouses ponder their position in marriage? The answer is worth!

People of all backgrounds have wondered about their worth. At some point we all have questioned our value to others. I'm sure you've speculated if current or past occupations offered adequate appreciation. If you have deliberated your estimation in the eyes of others, you stand among the ranks of the many not the few.

However, allow me to extend this reality. Your worth is not discovered in the decision of others; it is deeply rooted in the living God. God created you and He alone determines your value.

Many people will read my words of encouragement and quickly agree. Albeit, there will be some who will remain discouraged and find it difficult to conceive their worth. If you stand among the discouraged doubting your destiny, contemplating calling it quits, this chapter is for you.

Beloved, it's time for you to discover *whose you are* by

allowing "Him" to uncover *who He is* so you may recover what you've lost. I believe a pass and review of the patriarch Moses will allow us to accomplish this goal.

You Must Discover

Moses' life began in confusion and contradictions. At the time of his birth, the command of death was placed over all the Jewish male infants (Exod. 1:22). So from his very conception, the time when he should have been celebrated and placed on display, Moses was hidden. (Read Exodus 2.)

When Moses' mother could no longer hide him indoors she constructed a vehicle to conceal him outdoors. With a mother's love she designed a baby's basket not made of silk or satin, but of slime and sticks. Moses was placed in his basket in the river not to be seen, but to remain undetected through dirt and brush.

Why would his mother place him in an ark of no value? Could it be she lacked affection for her child? We must not search the vehicle he traveled in; we must focus on the environment he traveled through to get our answer. The river had to be filled with alligators, snakes, and many other deadly amphibians. A beautiful basket might have brought unwanted attention. Mindful of pending danger, Moses' mother dressed his ark not to show affection but to provide protection.

As he traveled down the river, Moses was eventually discovered by the daughter of Pharaoh. She adopted the Hebrew baby as her own. However, rather than allowing Moses to develop with a sense of pride for his nationality, he was forced to pretend to be an Egyptian. In essence, Moses was trained in the art of artifice. He was taught early in his life his people were worthless.

Although he was trained to believe his true ethnicity held

no value, his mother was paid wages to nurse him. One could argue this was the first record of child support. Now, I'm sure Moses' mother secretly taught him Jewish pride. Therefore, when he was old enough he killed an Egyptian for mistreating a fellow Hebrew.

What brought this otherwise mild man to the point of murder? Maybe it was the years of covering up his true identity. It could have been pent up frustrations stemming from being made to feel his social class, culture and customs were worthless.

After committing murder, Moses fled the scene and found himself on the backside of the desert (Exod. 3:1). Although Moses was raised in the family of the king of Egypt, he was lacking what mattered most—identity. Even at his wealthiest moment, Moses felt worthless.

How about you? In your early developing years were you celebrated or tolerated. Even now when you share your thoughts or emotions, have you felt the sting of rejection or ridicule? If so, it's imperative you know the pain and problems were all in God's plan.

Like Moses, you may find yourself on the backside—I'm talking so far back you think no one sees you. However, you need to know God's looking right in your direction. He's waiting for you to discover your identity is not found in what others think or say about you. Your identity is in what He thinks and says about you.

Now hear this; the Almighty God, possessor of the heavens and the earth, has you on His mind (Ps. 8:4; 139:17; Jer. 29:11). If that doesn't cause you to lift your head and recognize your worth, nothing will. Truth is, the only way you'll really discover your worth is not trying to discover who you are, but *whose* you are.

God Will Uncover

In Exodus 3 Moses' story continues. One day while Moses was tending his flock, he noticed something extremely peculiar. In the distance Moses saw a bush on fire and yet it was not consumed.

While Moses turned to investigate the bush, God was ready to investigate his life. The Lord called Moses' name twice. This is significant because it meant God was ready to uncover Himself after He exposed the cover-up of Moses.

In the Bible whenever we find God calling people's names twice, He's about to uncover some truth about Himself and the person to whom He's speaking. Consider the account with Abraham concerning God's covenant (Gen. 22:11). How about Martha concerning her cleaning (Luke 10:41)? Contemplate Saul who later became the Apostle Paul concerning his conversion (Acts 9:4). These are just a few examples of God calling people's names twice in order to uncover something concealed.

Has God been trying to get your attention? Does He need to call your name twice in order to uncover a truth that's right in front of you? The Lord wants you to know your importance. He's willing to reach far regions to make you aware of your worth.

Back in Exodus 3 we read how the Lord instructed Moses to remove his shoes because the land he stood on was holy. Moses needed to remove the very thing that came between his hiding and God's holiness. The same feet that fled the scene in Egypt and traveled in desert places had to become bare in order for God to repair.

The Lord instructed Moses to go back with a message for Pharaoh. In essence, God confronted Moses so he could confront his past. Facing his past would allow him to embrace his future. However, as God made plans, Moses made excuses. Moses hung the mission on his humanity, but God was counting on His own divinity.

As God spoke to Moses concerning His plan of deliverance, Moses did what he was so accustomed to—hiding. Moses' true struggle was not with God; it was with himself.

Moses had no self-worth and thought the Pharaoh would see no value in his presence. He asked God the question many of us ask in our quiet times or our isolated moments. He simply asked, "Who am I?" (v. 11). Rather than confirming Moses' identity God uncovered His own.

Finally, Moses asked the question that mattered most; the question that would alter the course of his life and release Israel from subjugation. With humility Moses enquired of God's name; and the Lord revealed, "I Am That I Am!" (v. 14). This name emphasized God's dynamic and His active self-existence. In essence, the Lord is worth knowing and having Him around adds new meaning to our lives.

Have you discovered the Lord is more than enough? No matter what you face, it pales in comparison to His power. God is all you need to succeed in life. However, you'll never discover God is all you need until He is all you have. This is why the Lord reveals Himself to us. With the Lord we can do all things (Phil. 4:13), but without Him we can do nothing (John 15:5).

Like Moses, we desperately need the Lord to uncover His identity because it's His significance that gives our lives worth. The combination to success is in knowing first, "Who He is"; and second, acknowledging "We are His." Once this happens we are ready to recover all that we lost.

You Can Recover

From the time of his birth, Moses lost his identity. He went from being a Hebrew to being an Egyptian by no choice of his own. I'm sure there were times among the Egyptians when he felt like the odd man out. We do know that when he matured he refused to be called the son of Pharaoh's daughter (Heb. 11:24).

While experiencing a life of leisure, Moses was lost. He lost himself as a person, he lost his people, and he lost his passion. However, while living as a castaway God called his name.

God will call the misplaced. Although He's seated high, the Lord will take the time to come low. He is never far from us. He sees our tears, hears our cries, and knows our sorrows (Exod. 3:7). He told Moses, "I am come down to deliver..." (v. 8). In essence, God declared He comes to help the lost recover.

In fact, when Jesus began His earthly ministry He went to the Jewish synagogue, opened the holy book, and began reading. He found where it was written and said in essence: "The Lord's Spirit is on me to preach the gospel to the poor, heal the broken hearted, preach deliverance to the captives, recovering of sight to the blind and to liberate the bruised" (Luke 4:18). This was His declaration of recovery!

God assigned Moses as lead spokesman of His rescue mission. He told Moses to instruct the leaders of Israel to prepare for recovery. But, the people of God had been oppressed so long they had become accustomed to their captivity. They sent out distress signals for four hundred years, but eventually lost hope. To them help became good conversation, yet they stopped anticipating a demonstration.

Moses received schooling in Egypt. He obtained the finest education, yet he lacked revelation. So, before he could talk for God he needed to be taught by God.

Moses was given a class on *his*tory. The Lord taught that He was the God of Abraham, Isaac and Jacob (Exod. 3:15). Moses was schooled in God's mathematics. God + No One Else = the Majority. Moses sat through the class of God's miracles (4:2–9). Finally, Moses was given God's speech lesson (vv. 10–12).

After being convinced that God's ability to succeed was greater than his inabilities, Moses set out to accomplish God's will. Through God's power Moses was able to recover God's people. Through it all he learned to rest in *who* He (God) is and was comforted in knowing he was His. Moses learned his greatest strength was the God who worked within him.

The Coca Cola Company had to learn a similar lesson. They thought by changing their formula they would increase their chances of success in the consumer market. However, they learned in a matter of months not to tamper with the original formula, not even to keep up with the ever changing trends.

When the announcement was made public in July of 85' that Coca Cola was returning to their old formula, it was met with nationwide approval. The news found its way in every major newspaper in the country. The Coca Cola Company started a campaign advertising the old formula as "Coca Cola Classic." With the return of the original formula sales soared and both the company and consumers were ecstatic.[5]

Friend, our worth is not found in the world; our worth is found in our God. No matter what we face in life learn, like Moses and Coca Cola, the power we have within is greater than any pressure we experience without (1 John 4:4).

It's time to discover that God will uncover so we can recover all the enemy has taken. Our worth is in knowing, "Who He is and I am His!"

Remember, God will turn your disability into His possibility because; He is the *worth* for the worthless!

Chapter 8
POINTS TO PONDER

God created you, and He alone determines your value. Write the four attributes of God's people found in 1 Peter 2:9:

_____

_____

_____

_____

God has you on His mind (Ps. 8:4; 139:17; Jer. 29:11). Now write how that makes you feel.

_____

Has God ever spoken to you? What did He say?

_____

_____

According to the chapter, what is the combination to success?

_____

_____

Like Moses and Coca Cola, what do you need to learn?

_____

_____

Some friends may ruin you, but a real friend will be more loyal than a brother.

—PROVERBS 18:24, NCV

9

Friend for the Friendless
You're Welcomed

A S A CHILD I can recall seeing an educational commercial which brought awareness to the issue of prejudice. The commercial took place in a park where two boys of different ethnicities were talking. They appeared to have been playing softball because one was holding a bat while the other a glove and ball.

Their day and fun was cut short because of approaching inclement weather. Not wanting their time together to end, one boy said to the other, "Hey, let's go spend time at your house!" The other boy now looking down responded, "I don't think going to my house is a good idea. But, let's go to your house instead!" The first boy groaned, "I know my house wouldn't work." The commercial concluded with both boys disappointedly standing in the middle of the park.

They were able to play together away from the demands and negative distractions of life. However, a figurative door stood between them having a close friendship. At the threshold of this door lay a mat that read, Not Welcomed.

Apparently at home each boy was given the harsh concept of prejudice. Personally, this was not their philosophy, but unfortunately it was their reality. Inward shame caused an outward shunning whereby these boys came short of truly sharing.

Rejection is the Achilles heel of any relationship. The natural reaction to rejection is to become withdrawn, aloof, and uninterested in moving forward. Being unwelcomed in any situation is not a good feeling, and it certainly isn't ideal when it comes to developing friendships.

I have had moments when I felt unwelcomed. In those situations I would have appreciated having a friend there for comfort and support. Friends do just that! They give us comfort and encouragement. We never have to monitor our thoughts or measure our words with a friend. We are free to share our deepest thoughts without fear of being judged or having them spread all over social media.

Jesus is that kind of friend. He says to the weary, wounded and most of all unwelcomed, "Come" (Matt. 11:28). He's never in short supply of love. He beckons to the brokenhearted, He invites the victims, and He faces the friendless with a smile of adoration.

We're never without a friend in this world where God is concerned. He is a friend to all who feel friendless. And as a friend we have God's attention, assistance, and acceptance.

WE HAVE GOD'S ATTENTION

God desires to be our friend. In fact, He's so bent on friendship that He thinks about us every day. His thoughts of us are good not evil and He has plans to bring us through every trial we face (Jer. 29:11). Isn't that the DNA of friendship? Friends think fondly of each other.

It should make you warm inside knowing you have God's

attention. The Bible records God is mindful of us (Ps. 8:4). In the myriad of duties that confront the Lord, nothing takes precedence over His love for us. Even more than His love is the attention He gives us.

Like us, Abraham became the object of God's devotion. And like us, Abraham did not warrant God's affection and he certainly was not worthy of His attention.

Abraham came from a regular family. He was not born into royalty nor was he blessed with unusual talent. God's attention was on Abraham, *not* because he was special; Abraham was special because he had God's attention. The first part of Abraham's journey is in Genesis 12 and 13.

God spoke to Abraham with instructions to come out from his family and familiar surroundings. God promised to add quality and quantity to Abraham's life. The Lord gave Abraham a promise of provision, protection, and posterity.

Why was Abraham given all this attention? We already noted he couldn't earn it of his own accord, Abraham was bankrupt. When it came to money, he had none. If you looked for a charming personality, he didn't stand out. Was he a genius? Well, let's just say the Bible didn't mention it. If none of the aforementioned granted Abraham God's attention, what could it be? I submit to you the Lord gave His attention because He's a friend who sticks closer than a brother (Prov. 18:24).

If I can say anything about Abraham, I will say this: he reciprocated God's attention by devoting time to God as well. His account reads like a budding relationship in the courting phase. Throughout his walk with the Lord Abraham built altars. Abraham's altars represented his devotion to God and his commitment to hearing God speak.

Do you want God's attention? If so, build some altars. Your

altars don't have to be built with your hands; God is looking for the altar of your heart. The scripture above reveals if a person desires friends they must be friendly. In essence, if we want God's attention we must be willing to offer Him ours. As a friend, God gives us His attention. Even more, He gives us His assistance.

WE HAVE GOD'S ASSISTANCE

Having God's assistance is wonderful. There's nothing we cannot accomplish with the help of God. Every challenge we face, every adversary we encounter is rendered useless because the Lord is our helper (Heb. 13:6).

Abraham learned firsthand about the help of God. The Lord made a covenant with Abraham (Gen. 15). Notice it was the Lord Who made a covenant with Abraham and not the other way around. For this reason, I would like to clarify what a covenant is and what it is not.

First, a covenant is higher than a contract. A contract stipulates, "If you do then I'll do." Albeit, a covenant emphatically states, "I—will—do!" Allow me to further my point. When God spoke with Moses concerning His people, He issued the Law. The Law was God's contract. The Law specified if the people did their part in obeying, God would do His part by blessing them. Thus, "If you do then I will do."

Now let's look at covenant. When God approached Abraham He made a covenant with him (Gen. 15). God told Abraham how He would bless him without inhibitions. God never told Abraham he had to do anything to receive the blessings; they would come strictly from God's part. In essence, God conveyed: "I will do!"

Let's continue to compare God's contract and His covenant. When God delivered His contract (Law), there were a lot of external demonstrations that connected with people performing duties. On that day there were thunders, lightning, a thick cloud, a loud trumpet, smoke, fire, earth shaking, people trembling (Exod. 19:16–18). The whole event was a demonstration of God's power.

Above all, the people had to perform duties. In order to prepare for God's appearance, they were to clean their bodies, clean their clothes (v. 10), place borders between them and God (vv. 12–13), and abstain from sexual relations with their spouses (v. 15).

Now consider the account with Abraham. God approached Abraham; there were no borders or barriers. God didn't choose the method of a mediator like in the case of His contract (Moses speaking to the people). God elected to speak to Abraham personally—the action of a friend.

When God offered His assistance to Abraham through the giving of His covenant, there were no external demonstrations only internal determinations. The Lord was showing His love.

Although Abraham had to meet God's requirement (Gen. 17:1) within God's contract, he didn't have to make any promises of his own to receive God's covenant. God simply told Abraham to place certain animals on the ground and cut them in two halves in order to solidify the covenant. This was a ritual performed by the Jews called "cutting covenant" (Jer. 34:18–19).

Please don't miss the beauty of all this and how it pertains to God's people today. When we have a covenant relationship with God, we can reveal our heart to Him. This is what Abraham did. He was so secure in his friendship with the Lord that he revealed the deep desire of his heart—an heir (Gen. 15:2).

The Lord then promised to make Abraham a father of many

and that his descendants would be countless (v. 5). The Bible records after Abraham received God's covenant (promise of assistance) he attempted to work in order to keep the covenant alive. Abraham labored throughout the day, but it was when he rested the Lord was able to do His part (Gen. 15:9–18).

My friend, receive now the help of the Lord. Understand when you have God's assistance you do not have to lift a hand; you just need to lift your eyes (Ps. 121:1–2). For many people accepting help is difficult. Even still, the Lord is a present help in the time of need (46:1). Quit trying to work out your issues and trust the Lord to work them out for you.

Are you ready to accept God's assistance? Even better, ponder this profound point: God has accepted you.

We Have God's Acceptance

Often we are taught that acceptance comes with a price. If we want to attend the prestigious universities, our transcripts must reflect academic excellence. Many exclusive clubs ostracize mainstream society for the social elite. Nowadays just finding a job is difficult because many companies spend enormous amounts of money on the vetting process. With so much scrutiny and suspicion, acceptance seems a rare commodity.

It's great to know that when it comes to God acceptance is not hard to find. In fact, God offers His acceptance with no strings attached. Now don't confuse acceptance with approval. God will always accept who we are, but He doesn't always approve what we do. This was the case with Abraham.

The Lord promised Abraham descendants; however, Abraham thought God needed assistance in making the promise good. Abraham's wife Sarah was incapable of childbearing. Therefore, they thought it wise for Abraham to father a child with Sarah's slave girl Hagar.

Once Hagar birthed a child for Abraham, she immediately despised Sarah for not being able to do the same. At this point, Abraham and Sarah realized their error in judgment. Nevertheless, God stepped in to help His friend out. Instructions were given to Abraham in order to rectify the situation.

God revealed His plan that Abraham and Sarah would have a child together. Abraham found God's plan preposterous so he laughed (Gen. 17:17), and later after hearing and entertaining tales of a toddler Sarah laughed (18:12). They laughed because they found it difficult to accept God's truth. Even when they didn't accept God's plan, the Lord accepted them. In the end the Lord got the last laugh (21:6). The couple named their son Isaac, which means "laughter."

Has God given you a promise that's difficult to accept? If you have been drowning in a sea of debt, the Lord can walk on water and pull you out. If you are lost in a cave of depression, the Lord shines the way out. If your marriage is spiraling toward divorce, the Lord provides the willpower to work it out. No matter the situation, God gets the last laugh and you're left smiling with Him.

Typically, life's no laughing matter, but we can learn to laugh in life. We laugh because we have God's love and it's His love that lifts us in any situation.

There's nothing we ever did to warrant God's love; and there's nothing we can ever do to cancel His love. God is our Creator and He's made us in His image (Gen. 1:26). He not only made us, He has accepted us into His family (Eph. 1:6).

I hear someone saying, "I'm made in His image, but I've made many mistakes." Mistakes don't disqualify us because we're sometimes bad; mistakes should notify us that God is always good. God's acceptance is without conditions. He doesn't extend His welcome when we're good and retract it when we're bad. After all, Jesus taught we are to love our enemies (Matt. 5:44; Luke 6:35). Now think, we're not God's enemies, we're God's friends.

Abraham certainly made his share of mistakes. Abraham told his wife to lie because he was scared (Gen. 12:11–13). He listened to his wife over God and concocted a plan outside of God's will (16:2). On another occasion Abraham told a king Sarah was his sister (20:2). Actually, there were many times when Abraham missed the mark because he was not perfect. However, when the testimony of his life was recorded the conclusion read, "He staggered not at the promise of God and was strong in faith" (Rom. 4:20).

How do we justify the account given concerning Abraham's walk? We just read where Abraham missed it many times; however, he didn't miss God when it counted.

When God told Abraham to sacrifice his beloved son to show his true commitment, Abraham came through with flying colors. God accepted Abraham's sacrifice and provided for him a ram in the bush. For his sacrifice and more importantly his belief in the Lord, Abraham was called God's friend (James 2:23).

God said concerning Abraham, "I know Him" (Gen. 18:19; 22:12). It is one thing for us to say we know God and another altogether for God to announce He knows us. Jesus said there will be some who will claim to work in His name, but He will announce, "I never knew you" (Matt. 7:23). The Lord knows them that are His (2 Tim. 2:19). We belong to the Lord and when we follow Him He calls us friends (John 15:14).

My friend, are you currently struggling with a problem? Maybe you have an inward struggle, you feel would ostracize you from others. If so, go to God. He will never reject you.

He stands with open arms ready to embrace you with His love, shield you with His grace, extend His mercy and whisper, "You are welcomed."

Remember, God will turn your disability into His possibility because; He is the *friend* to the friendless!

Chapter 9
POINTS TO PONDER

Do you consider yourself a friend of God? _____
Explain your answer:

_____

_____

Are you in need of God's attention? _____
Write the concerns you need God to meet:

_____

_____

_____

Explain the difference between a covenant and a contract:

_____

_____

_____

Has God made a promise to you? What is it?

_____

_____

Now find scriptures relating to His promise and write them here:

_____

_____

Now rehearse God's Word over your issue(s).

After I go and prepare a place for you, I will come back and take you to be with me so that you may be where I am.

—JOHN 14:3, NCV

10

Home for the Homeless

A Place Prepared for You

I N 1976 A vision was birthed in two people that would liter-
ally change the landscape of the world. Millard and Linda
Fuller walked away from a lucrative business and a lavish
lifestyle. They found a new desire to seek spiritual fulfillment
in service to their Christian faith.

A small community outside of Americus, Georgia, named
Koinonia Farm was where the Fullers teamed up with the
Farm's founder Clarence Jordan. The name Koinonia comes
from a Greek term, which means community or having all
things in common.[1] This is significant because this location
served as the birthing place for the Habitat for Humanity
International.[2]

The Habitat for Humanity International was a concept to
provide adequate and affordable housing for impoverished
people. The houses were constructed without the builders
receiving any profit. Also, the loans provided for the homes
came without interest. Koinonia Farm served as a launching
pad for this sincere endeavor. The farm donated forty-two

half-acre sites for housing and a recreational park. Resources
were received nationwide to commence the project.[3]

In time the project manifested into a global mission. Later,
the Fullers decided to use the Habitat for Humanity concept
to build housing in underdeveloped countries.[4]

Eventually in 1984 the Habitat for Humanity organization
found its biggest supporters in former U.S. President Jimmy
Carter and his wife Rosalynn. Involvement from this powerful couple brought national visibility. Sponsors and supporters poured in from numerous places and the Habitat for
Humanity organization experienced phenomenal growth.[5]

The Fuller's noble act is certainly worthy of appreciation
and celebration. Their sacrifice and the efforts of many like
them have made it possible for the homeless to have a place
of their own.

It's a sad commentary to live in this world without a place
to call home. Yet that's exactly the predicament many people
find themselves. Having a home extends beyond a mortgage;
it's a mindset.

Where are you right now? Are you beyond difficulty living
home-free, destitute among the homeless, or somewhere in
between? Remember, the homeless is not merely a state of
being, it's a state of mind. Owning a house doesn't consti-
tute having a home. No matter the city, country, or continent,
home means having cover and finding comfort and a sense of
constancy.

The Lord wants all His people to know in Him we find
a home. He invites us to come live with Him and share His
address (John 14:2–3). And until we live with Him in eternity,
God steps into our time to provide a home for us now.

GOD GIVES US COVER

Every home provides cover. The Lord is our strong tower where the righteous run into and are safe (Prov. 18:10). The Lord is our shelter from the elements and our enemies (Ps. 61:3). In fact, the Bible tells us we can dwell in the secret place of God and abide under His shadow (Ps. 91:1–2). God provides the cover that His people need.

David became the second king of Israel. His legacy differs from Saul, the first king of Israel. Both men stepped onto the pages of history caring for their fathers' animals. Interestingly, the state of the animals revealed the condition in which each man would eventually find himself.

Saul was commanded by his father to locate lost donkeys (1 Sam. 9:3). Donkeys are known to be stubborn, and that's exactly what Saul became. He became a king that would not yield to God but would do things his own way. (See 1 Samuel 15.). On the other hand, David was commissioned by his father to take care of his sheep (1 Sam. 16:11). Sheep depend on their shepherd for protection. They get into trouble without the shepherd's guidance. Like sheep, David relied on God or he found himself in messy situations (sheep dip).

In reality, Saul was tall externally (1 Sam. 9:2) but small internally. David was small outwardly but big inwardly. The people chose Saul as king because he looked the part. God chose David as king because he had the heart (16:7).

God told the prophet Samuel to anoint Saul with a vial of oil (10:1). A vial is a man-made bottle, which represented that man had made Saul king. Conversely, God ordered the prophet Samuel to anoint David with a horn of oil (vv. 12–13). The horn came from an animal which was God-made. This indicated God made David king. Also, the horn of oil meant David had God's covering.

In his manhood David had the Lord's covering in battle and his victories outnumbered Saul's victories exponentially. As king, Saul was known for slaying thousands. Even before he became king, David was celebrated for killing tens of thousands (18:7). God's covering over David became obvious and this enraged Saul (vv. 8–9). For this cause David had to flee Saul's anger, and without warning he found himself homeless (19:18).

Maybe you have found yourself in a similar predicament. Has God's favor placed you on the wrong side of someone's temper? At work you excel, so others have singled you out as kissing up to the boss. God's influence has caused you to shine in life, and some people have made it their mission to keep you in the shadows.

If you have felt the sting of jealously or the tight grip of envy, don't complain; just stay under God's cover. The Lord will fight your battles and see to it you're vindicated of all wrong doing. Receive God's covering and feel His comfort.

God Gives Us Comfort

Every home provides comfort. David spent a lot of years running from King Saul. While living as a fugitive in the Judean wilderness, he penned the famous twenty-third psalm. In these six verses he expressed how he received the Lord's comfort.

David viewed himself as a sheep and announced the Lord to be his shepherd whereby he lacked nothing. In his desperate condition he spoke of how the Lord made him to lie down and rest beside still waters. Sheep are fragile and the slightest noise can disturb their rest. David continued to express how even in the valley of the shadow of death he had no fear because the Lord was present.

David spoke of the Lord preparing his table in the midst of his enemies. Also, he remembered the Lord anointed his head with oil. Again, this spoke of the Lord's presence with David. Finally, David thought of God's goodness and mercy in his life. Therefore David declared that he would dwell in the house of the Lord forever.

While in a homeless state of being, David chose not to have a homeless state of mind. He dreamed of being in the Lord's house. Although he was on the run, he knew how to find rest. His rest was in the Lord!

My friend, the Lord will give you comfort because He is your comfort. If you find yourself in a tough situation, don't focus on the problem but focus on the Lord. When you look at the problem you'll see a crisis; when you look at the Lord you'll receive His comfort.

For some people the crisis is their crop. When I say crop, I mean they caused the problem to occur. The Bible teaches we reap what we sow (Gal. 6:7). But I'm so thankful God provides the opportunity to reverse any curse we may have caused. This is what David discovered first hand when he wrote about the Lord's goodness and mercy.

Chapters 11 and 12 of 2 Samuel tell us of another story of David. After becoming Israel's king, David committed a horrible act. He committed adultery with a woman named Bathsheba. Bathsheba was married to Uriah, one of David's soldiers.

After discovering Bathsheba was pregnant with his child, David summoned Uriah home from war. David instructed Uriah to sleep with his wife in hopes to cover his transgression. However, Uriah was loyal and refused to take pleasure while his comrades fought in battle. David then conspired to have Uriah killed.

David eventually married Bathsheba and he sought the Lord's forgiveness for his sin. The Lord spared David's life but took the life of the child from their adulterous relationship. After receiving the news of his child's death, David anointed himself and went back to God's house. He knew God was his shelter in the midst of that storm.

Eventually, David and Bathsheba had a second son and called his name Solomon. The name Solomon means "Peace with God or God's Peace." God's prophet called the baby Jedidiah meaning "Beloved," because the Lord loved the child.

Although David made a grave mistake, he sought the Lord's forgiveness and received the Lord's comfort. When we bring God truth, He'll grant us mercy and the result is we'll have God's peace (Ps. 85:10).

God's loving kindness is better than life (63:3). Discovering this brings us comfort. The Lord is home to the homeless; and the greatest thing about home is it's always there.

GOD GIVES US CONSTANCY

Every home provides constancy. The almanac of David's life was filled with adventure and attrition. By adventure he lived the life of legends. By attrition he suffered much loss. The one constant in David's life; the One who was always there was God.

David faced off with lions, bears, massive men, and colossal armies. He changed wives as easily as he changed shirts. He lived among the desperate and destitute and commanded the company of mighty men. His exploits stand impressive when compared to any hero. Yet he was renowned for his humility.

David was no stranger when it came to taking a loss. He lost his dearest friend Jonathan to war (1 Sam. 31:2). His first wife was taken from him and given to another man (25:44). He lost the affection of his father-in-law who attempted to kill him on numerous occasions (19:1, 10–11). He lost his kingdom momentarily because he refused to fight his own son (2 Sam. 15:13–17). These are a few of his many losses. However, through it all God remained a constant fixture in David's life.

Whether you are a globe trotter or you tend to stay close to your local area, the wonderful thing about home is it's always there. This is our God! Through all the trials and triumphs, adversities and advantages, we can count on Him to be there for us.

God walks with us today. More importantly, He goes before us to ensure anything the enemy plans for us will not succeed (Ps. 139:5). This is what God did for young David when he faced a giant-sized man. However, David didn't fight the giant alone. David declared as the Lord had saved him from a lion and bear, God would save him from the giant (1 Sam. 17:37). David knew God was constant and would not let him down.

David choose five smooth stones (v. 40), but only used one stone on Goliath. This left David with four stones. Could it be David overestimated the task at hand? I don't think so. I believe the Lord intuitively had David select five stones, one for his present problem and four for his future fights.

Goliath was the first giant David had to fight, but he was not the last. Later, David fought and defeated four more giants (2 Sam. 21:15–22). Is this a coincidence? Maybe, but I don't think so.

With all these victories in battle, David could have easily become prideful; but this man remained humble. The reason for his humility is simple. The Bible records that David knew how to behave himself because the Lord was with him (1 Sam. 18:14).

The Lord goes before us and causes us to prepare for battles today and for those unforeseen tomorrow. The problems that appear now will dissipate later. However, the Lord is faithful. He's the same yesterday, today, and forever (Heb. 13:8).

The Lord is our shelter and He inspires organizations like Habitat for Humanity in the hearts of men.

Thousands of impoverished families have found decent affordable housing through the tireless efforts of the Habitat for Humanity organization. Different companies and government agencies as well as countless volunteers have joined in the relief efforts.

Since the inception of Habitat for Humanity International 6.8 million people have been given strength, stability and shelter.[6]

If one couple can initiate a movement to shelter millions of homeless, imagine what our mighty God can do. Jesus said He's preparing a place for us that where He is we may be also (John 14:2–3). The place Jesus spoke of is His Father's house; it's your Father's house—it's your home.

Remember, God will turn your disability into His possibility because; He is the *home* for the homeless!

Chapter 10
POINTS TO PONDER

Where are you right now? Are you beyond difficulty living home-free, destitute among the homeless, or somewhere in between? Explain your answer:

_____   _____

_____

Do you currently feel God's covering? Explain your reply:

_____

_____

What does it mean when your crisis becomes your crops?

_____

Have you ever experienced a crop and needed God's mercy?

_____

 If so, recall and record God's mercy in your life:

_____

_____

Where do you consider home? _____

Do you need covering, comfort, or constancy in your life?
If so, express it here then give it to God:

_____

_____

_____

_____

Without faith no one can please God.
Anyone who comes to God must believe
that he is real and that he rewards
those who truly want to find him.

—HEBREWS 11:6, NCV

11

Faith for the Faithless

Trust Him Anyhow

I N THE SUMMER of 2009, my wife and I decided to provide our daughter Jada with swimming lessons. I made
sure I was there every weekday morning to witness her
development. I paid for her classes and prayed for her safety
as I sat in the bleachers with the other proud parents.

There were various phases to the lessons, and like a pro Jada
mastered them all; well, all but one—diving. The instructor
told all the students to position themselves in a line, come to
the edge of the pool, and jump in. One student after the other
plunged in until they reached my "Olympian in the making."

When it was her turn at the edge of the pool, Jada resem-
bled a statue. The swim instructor yelled to Jada, "Jump in!"
Even still, Jada stood—Jada stared—Jada stalled. Again, the
instructor commanded, "Jump!" and like before, my baby girl
did not comply.

The instructor tried talking Jada through the operation;
no response. The coach allowed the other kids to perform
the task again so Jada could see it was easy; still she silently

objected. Finally, the time lapsed and the class concluded. When Jada returned to the bleachers to collect her items, she found me waiting with a huge hug and smile.

With sensitivity I enquired why she wouldn't jump in the pool, and with a sad countenance she admitted her fear. I quickly assured her that Daddy was close by watching and she was free from harm. Then I asked her if she trusted me. When she responded, "Yes," I told her to listen for my voice the next time she was in that position.

Like Jada, we have all experienced points and arrived at places where fear took control of us. Fear appears in multiple degrees. It starts as children with the proverbial monster in our closet. If not checked fear grows to the economy crashing, terrorist attacks, and deadly world viruses.

The only true remedy for fear is faith. Now, I'm not speaking of any kind of faith. Everyone has faith, but not everyone's faith is where it should be. People place faith in their physicians, politicians, government agencies, etc. However, our faith must always be in God.

The lives of three Hebrew boys will point to the importance of placing our faith in the living God. You see, true faith must be tested because a faith that cannot be tested cannot be trusted. Many people believe faith is designed to get them out of trouble. However, many times our faith in God gets us into trouble. Faith is not to get us out of trials; it's to get us through the trials.

Three Hebrew boys were made to change their customs, culture, language and among many other things, their names. Hananiah's Jewish name was switched to the Babylonian's Shadrach; Mishael was changed to Meshach, and Azariah was given the name Abednego (Dan. 1:7). These young men were willing to change many things, but one change was asking too much. They refused to change their God! Daniel 3 tells the story in detail.

A royal decree was given that whenever the Babylonian's played their music everyone must bow to the golden image the king had erected. If anyone failed to bow after hearing the music they were to be burned alive in a furnace of fire. The time came when the music was played but the three Hebrew boys refused to bow and regard the Babylonian gods or worship the golden image.

Now came the testing of their faith! The three Hebrew boys were brought before the enraged king. The sire demanded answers for their insolence. He asked the question that makes or breaks any Christian: "Who is the God that will deliver you out of my hands?" The devil will always tempt our faith to bring out our worse; God will always test our faith to bring out our best. In either case, just know your faith will be tested!

The Hebrew boys responded to the Babylonian king's demand with what I call the Believer's Creed. A creed is a principle. And in this case a principle we live by and, if necessary, die by. The Hebrews spoke with a resounding voice: "We have no need to answer you in this matter....Our God whom we serve is able to deliver us from the burning fiery furnace, and He will deliver us from your hand, O king. But if not, let it be known...we do not serve your gods, nor will we worship the golden image which you have set up" (Dan. 3:16–18, NKJV).

There are many reasons to fear, especially when you do not know the Lord. But the child of God has no cause for fear because the hell-stopper and problem-solver is on our side. The three Hebrew boys knew what every believer must come to know—the Lord is powerful, proven, and He won't be pressured.

The Lord Is Powerful

The Hebrew boys declared, "Our God is able to deliver us from the burning fiery furnace." First and foremost, their faith rested on God's ability. To recognize God's ability is to understand He has power beyond any problem, pain, or pressure we face. What's more, we're not to limit God's power to the point of our own.

Too many Christians give up and throw in the towel. They look at the negative circumstances presented and conclude nothing can be done. Any problem that's bigger than us is breeding ground for a miracle from God.

God looks for opportunities to give people of the world a lesson on His power and expose their weaknesses. Consider the account when Moses and Aaron defeated Pharaoh's magicians (Exod. 7–12); or when Elijah challenged the prophets of Baal on Mount Carmel (1 Kings 18); and don't forget the time when Paul exposed the false sorcerer (Acts 13:1–12). When the Babylonian king tested the Hebrew boy's faith, he enrolled in God's class of discipline. We can call it "Theology for Dummies!"

Only when we trust God's ability are we ready to receive His power. The Hebrew boys were facing immediate death, but their resolve not to betray their God was greater than the death threat. God gave them power from within to handle the pain and problems from without.

The Hebrew boys had to make the choice of becoming "conformers" or "transformers." God's Word admonishes us not to be conformed to this world but to be transformed (Rom. 12:2). To be conformed to this world means we are pressed into the world's forms, fashions, and figures. This is what was demanded of the people in the Babylonian region. And, conformity was the weight placed on the Hebrew boys.

People who conform are controlled by external factors; people who are transformed are controlled by their internal motivations. The Hebrew boys knew and placed their faith in the power of God's Word. When they faced the fire, they could have drawn from the scripture that says, "When you walk through fire, you will not be burned, nor will the flames hurt you" (Isa. 43:2, NCV).

There will be times when we'll need to know God is powerful. Even more, we must understand God is proven.

THE LORD IS PROVEN

After declaring God's power, the boys announced, "God will deliver us out of your hand, O King." In essence, these boys knew their God was a proven deliverer.

The Hebrew boys didn't operate from blind faith—not knowing God. They had strong faith knowing their God was not a novice, He was experienced in the delivering business. Every Jew was brought up and taught about the miracles of God. Every Hebrew father was under command to teach his children about God's power and the miracles He performed (Ps. 78:1–4).

Therefore, when facing the fire, the Hebrew boys were able to resort back to their teachings about the Lord. This is what God's people must do today. God's Word was written for our learning so that through patience we might find comfort and hope (Rom. 15:4). How do we find comfort and hope in the scriptures? We find it when we see God delivering His people from various predicaments.

When Israel had the armies of Egypt on their backs and the Red Sea blocking their front, God made a way where there was no way. When Israel trekked through the desert and came to the point of starvation and dehydration, God provided meal and drink. When the city of Jericho was fortified prohibiting Israel from obtaining the land promised, God crashed the walls and crushed the opposition.

Let's recall King Jehoshaphat and the nation of Judah while surrounded by their enemies. They had no power to fight, but they knew who had the power—God. Jehoshaphat sought God's help and the Lord defeated their enemies and released an abundance of wealth on Judah. Throughout the centuries God has proven Himself to be greater than pharaohs, empires, armies, famines, plagues, nature and even our last enemy—death.

Time would fail before we could express all the Lord's exploits. Before time started and life existed the Lord was here. Jesus is the Alpha and Omega, the beginning and the end, the Ancient of Days, and our hope for tomorrow. He's the rock of our salvation and the foundation we must build our lives upon. To have faith in anyone or anything else above God is ludicrous, because our Lord is proven.

When we truly begin to comprehend our Lord's power and appreciate He is proven, we can relax knowing He won't be pressured.

THE LORD ISN'T PRESSURED

The Hebrew boys declared God's power. They announced He's proven. But the real test of their faith came when they showed He wouldn't be pressured. By faith they proclaimed, "Even if God doesn't deliver us, we won't bow down and worship your gods."

Now, for many followers of God this is where the rubber meets the road. Can we place our faith in God without giving

Him a deadline to meet our demands? God is supernatural. This means He's not restricted to physical things nor is He governed by time. Therefore, we need to know the Lord will allow the deadline to pass. He'll allow the finances to deplete. God will even permit the people we count on to walk away so He may reveal *His* control.

The Hebrew boys informed the Babylonian king that they didn't serve a compulsive God. They gave God the liberty to operate on His timetable not theirs. The king, like the devil, breathes threats. The devil will attempt to terrorize us. He tells us if God doesn't show up our doom is inevitable. However, God doesn't negotiate with terrorists.

If need be, God will allow us to go through the passage of pain in order to show our passion for Him is greater than our pleasures in the world. Consider some of the acts of God's heroes of faith.

While under torture, they refused to submit to evil but chose to die and receive God's resurrection. Others underwent abuse such as whips and chains while they remained in dungeons. God's faithful people were stoned, sawed in two, and outright murdered. Many of the Lord's followers lived destitute, afflicted, and as wanderers (Heb. 11:35–38). The most puzzling testimony of all, the Bible records they had a good report even though they didn't receive their promise (v. 39).

Now, a man of no understanding would question God's power to perform. He might even ask why God wouldn't save His believers from this world's burdens. Well, the answer to these inquiries is found also in Scripture. God has provided something better for us; something bigger than escape (v. 40).

The time came when the three Hebrew boys were placed into the fire. The king with his host was waiting to hear screams.

They were expecting to see scorched bodies. Instead, they witnessed the Lord walking with His saints (Dan. 3:23–25).

Beloved, God may not deliver you from your trial the way you think He should, but you can count on Him walking with you in your trial. God could have delivered the Hebrew boys the way they declared He could. However, He had a bigger and better plan in mind. His plan was not to show He's the God who saves from the fire; He wanted the king to see He's the God who walks in the fire.

Remarkably, the Bible records the king saw Jesus, but it never indicated the Hebrew boys saw Jesus. Are you willing to go through trials so others may see God even if you don't see the Lord? Eventually, the boys were removed from the fire without their skin being burned or their clothes being singed (vv. 26–27). Have faith in God and you will recover without any evidence of going through your trial.

This king began asking, "Who is your God?" However, when God's class concluded, he confessed that God delivers His servants who trust in Him! (Dan. 3:28). The Lord is not pressured to perform because He always has the big picture in mind.

I started this chapter with the account of my daughter Jada who faced the daunting task of diving into a swimming pool. She was learning how to swim and had excelled in every facet of her lesson. However, when it came to performing the task of jumping in the water, fear gripped her heart.

After seeing no one could convince Jada to leap in the pool, I approached her with one question: "Do you trust Dad?" Jada confirmed she did trust me, so I told her to listen for my voice the next time she had to dive.

When the time for Jada to dive into the pool arrived again, her instructor ordered her to jump. Jada didn't move. Her classmates tried to encourage her to jump. Still, Jada didn't budge. Then I stood on the bleachers nearby and called Jada's name; when she looked my way, I said with a firm reassuring voice, "Jada, jump!" To everyone's surprise, Jada took a leap of love.

The Bible reveals that love believes all things (1 Cor. 13:7). Jada not only loves me, more importantly, she knows I love her. Therefore, Jada dove into the pool by faith. Since that moment Jada has developed as a swimmer and a diver. She now competes in the city league. She has won all kinds of awards; but the greatest award she has given me is her faith in me as her father.

God is our Father, and the greatest reward we can give Him is our faith in Him. We must have faith regardless of the feelings within us, the fights and fires around us because we focus only on the God above us.

Remember, God will turn your disability into His possibility because He is the *faith* for the faithless!

Chapter 11
POINTS TO PONDER

Are you currently coping with fear? If so, explain the remedy of fear:

_____

According to Daniel 3:16–18, write the believer's creed:

_____

_____

_____

How do you recognize God's ability/power?

_____

_____

Do you conform or are you transformed? Explain:

_____

_____

Has God proven Himself in your life? Explain:

_____

_____

According to the chapter, what is meant by God is supernatural?

_____

Do you know Him as the supernatural God? If so, explain:

_____

_____

_____

And I pray that you and all God's holy people will have the power to understand the greatness of Christ's love—how wide and how long and how high and how deep that love is.

—EPHESIANS 3:18, NCV

12

Love for the Loveless
Jesus Was Cross-Eyed

O NE OF MY top five romantic movies of all time is *Titanic*. Now, I know this opening statement appears to be an oxymoron. After all, the actual account of the *Titanic* was a tragic event. However, James Cameron the writer and director of the 1997 film placed a romantic twist on the well-known disaster.

The R.M.S. *Titanic* was the boast of the White Star Line.[1] In fact, the ship was the largest moving object on the ocean during its era.[2] As a luxurious liner it was affectionately referred to as the "Ship of Dreams."[3]

However, just before midnight on April 14, 1912, the colossal craft hit an iceberg and received detrimental damage. Large amounts of water entered the ship and eventually flooded the entire vessel. Nearly three hours later the *Titanic* sank to the bottom of the North Atlantic Ocean. Over 1,500 people were reported to have died in the icy waters.[4]

According to Cameron's version, in the midst of the devastation two young lovers found true devotion. Their relationship was deemed forbidden due to drastic differences in their social classes. The young man, Jack Dawson, was a penniless artist. The young lady, Rose Dewitt Bukater, was an aristocrat. However, against all odds, their love for each other prevailed.

As the ship was sinking and the remaining passengers panicking, Jack and Rose managed to position themselves at the ship's stern. As they braced themselves, the massive vessel plunged into the ocean. Amazingly, the two survived the ship's horrifying immerse.

While in the frigid water they found temporary refuge among the ship's wreckage. Jack placed Rose on a piece of board large enough for one person. Other surviving passengers were in the water struggling to stay afloat and screaming for help.

While Jack was in the water, and Rose barely positioned on the board, they firmly held hands. She told Jack she was cold and feared death was inevitable. Then Jack made Rose promise to hold onto life. He reassured her she would not die that night and told her she would live a long fulfilled life.

While shivering in the ocean and hypothermia setting into his body, Jack requested of Rose, "Promise me you'll survive. That you won't give up, no matter what happens, no matter how hopeless. Promise me now…and never let go." Rose quivered and in a soft whisper vowed, "I promise.…I'll never let go."[5]

Jack eventually died of hypothermia, but Rose survived and was rescued.

Cameron's tale of the *Titanic* was both heartbreaking and heartfelt. Is it possible to find love in tragedy? Is it conceivable to discover passion in pain? Not only is it possible, it is powerful and it has been done.

Jesus' crucifixion on the cross was the greatest devastation to occur on earth. Yet it stands as the highest demonstration of God's love for humanity. Now allow me to convey something that may appear disrespectful, but in truth reveals my reverence and deepest appreciation to our Lord. *Jesus was cross-eyed!* Every experience He encountered, every person He engaged, He did so with the cross in sight.

Jesus' love for us is without question the ultimate affection we can ever receive. We often hear authentic love has no conditions, and that's true. However, it's true because Jesus accomplished the primary condition for us—the cross. Now love has no conditions only provisions!

If you are living today and find it difficult to find authentic love, you're looking in the wrong place. God is love (1 John 4:8) and He sent His Son to demonstrate His undying love for us. In Jesus we discover the method and measure of love. And only after we learn the method and measure of love are we able to live with the mark of love.

God's Method of Love

Many people misunderstand God's love. They have diminished His love to an emotion. God's love goes beyond an emotion. His love is an act; and not just any act, but the ultimate expression of devotion.

Men have used all kinds of methods to express devotion. Worldwide, the heart is the symbolic shape used to express love. The heart has been placed on greeting cards, promoted on Valentine's Day, and used at numerous events. However, God does not recognize this shape for love.

God uses the cross to express His love; therefore, the cross counteracts the heart. Men use the heart as a symbol of love and a statement of comfort. The love men seek is comfortable and convenient. However, God's love bespeaks sacrifice and submission.

Jesus displayed sacrifice and submission in the garden of Gethsemane. Gethsemane is a Greek word that means oil press.[6] Jesus was pressed at Gethsemane, and it was there He agonized the night before His crucifixion on the cross. As Jesus prayed, He pleaded with God to release Him from the assignment of the cross. However, authentic love—God's love—has no escape plan.

Jesus' prayer was not to deny or change God's will. It was a display of His obedience and submission to the Father. Jesus finalized His prayer by saying, "Your will be done" (Matt. 26:42, NKJV). The method of love is not taking the easy way out. Love gives us no way out!

The Bible records Jesus endured the cross because of the joy that was before Him (Heb. 12:2). He endured the cross; He didn't enjoy it. However, we were the focal point of His joy. Remarkably, when Jesus walked with humanity all He saw was the cross—while He hung on the cross all He saw was humanity.

God's method of love was the pathway of pain. This is the passion of Christ. Just think, there would be no wine without crushed grapes and no bread without the beating of wheat. Likewise, we could not experience God's love without the cruelty of the cross. Knowing God's method of love had a high price should raise its value in our eyes.

Comprehending the method of God's love is just the beginning. To obtain a profound appreciation of our Lord means learning the measure of God's love.

GOD'S MEASURE OF LOVE

To say the measure of God's love is really misleading because it cannot be quantified. God's love has no boundaries and it breaks all barriers. His love is an international passport with an expiration date of infinity.

God's love reaches every custom, culture, ethnicity, and gender. There's no getting around the love of God, through the love of God, under the love of God, or over the love of God (Eph. 3:18). His love never ends (1 Cor. 13:8). The depth of God's love was the giving of His Son and the breadth of God's love reaches everyone.

The measure of God's love is His reach. Do you feel you're beyond the reach of God? Do you wonder if anyone cares? Well, the measure of God's love is endless. God not only cares about you, He loves you enough to meet you where you are and bring you where He is.

The Bible emphatically declares Jesus had to go through Samaria (John 4:4). To appreciate Jesus' itinerary included Samaria, you'll need to know the Jews and Samaritans were sworn enemies. The Jews considered the Samaritans a mixed breed stained by foreign blood and polluted with false worship.

So Jesus going through Samaria was not only a surprise to His disciples but an affront to their religion. However, Jesus was not concerned with religion; He looked for relationships. And there was a native woman of Samaria who desperately needed a relationship with the living God.

Following the account in John 4, we find Jesus was walking with His disciples when suddenly He became weary on His journey. His followers volunteered to refresh their Master by finding something to eat. While they were gone Jesus positioned Himself on a well.

It didn't take long for the Samaritan woman to approach Jesus at the well with her water pot in hand. The woman had every intention to draw from the well, but Jesus had designs to pour God's love into her.

First, Jesus requested water from the woman. Surprised by His request, she made remarks concerning their social differences. Smoothly, Jesus replied she should have asked Him for a drink. Intrigued, the woman inquired if His water was better than that from Jacob's well.

Continuing the conversation Jesus said His water satisfies forever. Persuaded by His words, the woman asked Jesus for this wonder water. Suddenly Jesus shifted the discussion to her love life. He inquired of her husband and she admitted she was not married. Jesus then revealed His point.

He recounted her broken marriages that exposed her failed attempts at love. Finally, Jesus proclaimed to be the very One she had been looking for (v. 26). Jesus is God's love personified. He went to great lengths for her and goes to great lengths for us no matter our setting.

The cultural setting of that day was not pleasant for women, especially a woman of her sort. This woman was despised because of her ethnicity; denounced because of her religion, and dejected because of her gender. However, Jesus didn't see her condition, He saw the cross. God's love touched and gave her significance (v. 39). Once the woman realized who Jesus was she left her water pot. She was no longer thirsty she was thankful.

Wherever you may be right now, don't miss God's love. Don't disqualify yourself on the bases of religion, race, culture, class, gender, or age; because the measure of God's love is great. Whether we ascend to heavenly places or descend in hellish locations, God's love can reach, hold, and help us (Ps. 139:8–10).

The method and measure of God's love is given so we may operate with His mark.

GOD'S MARK OF LOVE

God wants to leave an indelible mark on our lives. The mark He wants us to share is love.

In order to express the measure of God's love, we looked at the Samaritan woman. In particular, we examined how God's love would dare go beyond borders, reach pass religion, and touch the untouchable. However, the evidence of having God's love is found in how we love others (1 John 4:11–12). Are we able to reach past our differences and love each other the same way God loves us? This is an important question and a challenge presented to Jesus.

In Luke 10 we read of a lawyer who questioned Jesus about eternal life. Jesus responded to this lawyer concerning the Law. After all, a lawyer should have known God's law. The lawyer quoted the Shema of Israel: love God and your neighbor as you love yourself (Deut. 6:4–5; Luke 10:27).

After the lawyer finished reciting the Shema of Israel, Jesus said, "Do this and you will live." The lawyer understood to love God, but he pressed Jesus with another question. He asked, "Who is my neighbor?" (v. 29).

Our neighbors aren't only those who are like us, or even better, those we like; our neighbors are also those unlike us and people we don't like. Loving our neighbor is the true mark of love. To make this point Jesus tells the account of the Good Samaritan (vv. 30–35).

A certain man traveled from Jerusalem and came into Jericho where he was roughed up by thieves.

A priest passed by this wounded Jew but had no compassion. Then there was a Levite (a church leader). He stopped long enough to look at the wounded man, but offered no assistance. Finally, there was a Samaritan (a despised rival), who exemplified compassion, and ministered to the fallen man's needs. The Good Samaritan had the mark of love.

After telling the account of the Good Samaritan to His listeners, Jesus instructed them to go and do the same (vv. 36–37). Jesus always had the cross in His eyes and He wants us to have the cross in ours also.

The Apostle Paul laid an indictment against God's people when he said many are enemies of the cross (Phil. 3:18). To be an enemy of the cross means you desire comfort and convenience over sacrifice and suffering. However, when it comes to people, we must be longsuffering. After all, God is longsuffering with us. Paul was qualified to speak on this matter because he bore the marks of the Lord (Gal. 6:17). His marks revealed his love for God, and consequently, God's people.

Many of God's people are arguing and not loving each other. There are more debates over conviction than displays of compassion.

Make no mistake, the cross was cruel. It was devastating, but in all the ugliness you'll find devotion. It's been said that the Roman nails did not hold Jesus on the cross; His love did.

In the movie *Titanic*, Jack knew he was going to die but demanded his beloved Rose to live a fulfilled life. Through the tragedy of the cross we too can discover fulfillment. Jesus died for us so we may live for Him. He was cross-eyed, and now we can be cross-eyed, too.

Remember, God will turn your disability into His possibility because Jesus is the *love* for the loveless!

Chapter 12
POINTS TO PONDER

Have you felt God's love? If so, explain:

_____

_____

Explain God's method of love:

_____

_____

_____

Explain God's measure of love:

_____

_____

_____

Do you express God's mark of love? If so, explain:

_____

_____

_____

According to the chapter, what does it mean to say Jesus was cross-eyed?

_____

_____

Are you cross-eyed?

Notes

CHAPTER 2
HELP FOR THE HELPLESS

1.   John J. Parsons, "Hebrew Names of God," *Hebrew for Christians*, http://www.hebrew4christians.com/Names_of_G-d/El/el.html (accessed June 10, 2016).

CHAPTER 3
LIFE FOR THE LIFELESS

1.   "Why Bread is a healthy choice," Nutrition and Wellness, *Gardenia*, http://www.gardenia.com.ph/index.php/wellness/113-why-bread-is-a-healthy-choice.html (accessed June 10, 2016).

CHAPTER 4
REST FOR THE RESTLESS

1.   "Tetelestai—It is Finished! Paid in Full!" *preceptaustin* (blog), April 5, 2013, https://preceptaustin.wordpress.com/2013/04/05/tetelestai-it-is-finished-paid-in-full/ (accessed June 12, 2016).

CHAPTER 8
WORTH FOR THE WORTHLESS

1.   Conversations staff, "The Real Story of New Coke," *The Coca-Cola Company*, http://www.coca-colacompany.com/stories/coke-lore-new-coke/ (accessed June 14, 2016).
2.   Ibid.
3.   Ibid.
4.   Ibid.
5.   Ibid.

CHAPTER 10
HOME FOR THE HOMELESS

1.   *New Testament Greek Lexicon*, s.v. "*koinonia*," http://www.biblestudytools.com/lexicons/greek/kjv/koinonia.html (accessed June 15, 2016).

2. "The History of Habitat," *Habitat for Humanity*, http://www.habitat.org/how/historytext.aspx (accessed June 15, 2016).
3. Ibid.
4. Ibid.
5. Ibid.
6. Ibid.

CHAPTER 12
LOVE FOR THE LOVELESS

1. "Titanic," History.com, *A&E Television Networks*, http://www.history.com/topics/titanic (accessed June 16, 2016).
2. Ibid.
3. Old Rose (Frances Fisher) in the movie *Titanic*, written and directed by James Cameron, produced by Twentieth Century Fox Film Corporation, Paramount Pictures, Lightstorm Entertainment, et al., released December 19, 1997.
4. "Titanic," History.com.
5. Dialogue between Jack (Leonardo DiCaprio) and Rose (Kate Winslet) in the movie *Titanic*, written and directed by James Cameron, produced by Twentieth Century Fox Film Corporation, Paramount Pictures, Lightstorm Entertainment, et al., released December 19, 1997.
6. *Easton's Bible Dictionary*, s.v. "*Gethsemane*," http://www.biblestudytools.com/dictionaries/eastons-bible-dictionary/gethsemane.html (accessed June 16, 2016).

About the Author

TYRONE AND HIS wife, Andrea, have worked in full-time ministry for two decades. They serve under the tutelage of Bishop Nate Holcomb, the pastor and founder of Christian House of Prayer Ministries, Inc.

With a heart of compassion and a desire to impart learning, Tyrone Holcomb lays out the counsel of God with simplistic ease. He masterfully weaves biblical principles with humorous stories and witty phraseology that inspires laughter while enabling the listener to grasp and apply the truths of God's Word. Personal experience has taught him, "What life does to you depends on what life finds in you." Hence, his endeavor is to ensure always that Christ is found in all that he does.

Tyrone and Andrea's firm conviction is that God is straight, God is strong, and God won't leave you stranded. Therefore, they confidently conclude the will of God never takes us where His grace will not keep us.

Together this dynamic couple travels the country teaching and preaching the whole counsel of God.

Other Books by the Author

Is Your Marriage Healthy?

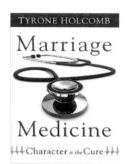

With so many marriages ending in divorce these days, you may wonder if love that lasts forever is a thing of the past. But take a closer look and you will see that many relationships fail not due to a lack of love but a lack of character.

Whether your marriage is on the rocks or you want to take your relationship to the next level, *Marriage Medicine* is just what the Doctor ordered.

Order Your Copy Today!

Make Your Marriage Matter More Than Ever Before.

Tap into the good life God has provided for marriages. In *Marriage Matters* author and minister Tyrone Holcomb shows readers how to apply God's Word to learn to love their spouse in a whole new way, thereby weathering the storms that will inevitably challenge anyone's marriage. Readers will be able to rekindle their love for their spouse through kindness, overcome struggles through patience, develop a "community of unity," and most importantly, strengthen the pillar of trust. By taking the love that God has freely given to believers and administering that same love to their spouses, readers can recapture the mandate for every believer—to love unconditionally. The result will be an unbreakable bond and a marriage steeped in the good life of God.

Order Your Copy Today!

MARRIAGE MATTERS: FOR BETTER OR FOR WORSE

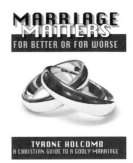

Every married couple and those considering marriage need to know their marriage will experience good and bad times. It's during the bad times that couples began to question whether their marriage is going to last. Perhaps you are now in that stage of inquiry. Don't give up! Instead, allow God to exhale on your marriage and witness it coming to life by every word that proceeds out of the mouth of God. Breath in—breath out—smile, your marriage will live and not die—*Marriage Matters.*

Order Your Copy Today!

BUILDING A LIFE OF LOVE TOGETHER

TYRONE HOLCOMB

Marriage

Maintenance

Better to Repair Than to Replace

"Marriage is a house of God's love," says pastor, Bible teacher, and counselor Tyrone Holcomb.

But, like any building, it can fall into disrepair if not looked after properly. The answer is not to demolish and start again or just patch things over. Rather, by restoring and remodeling, you can create the kind of wonderful home you always dreamed of.

Just turn to the Master Architect (Jesus).

Like a skilled contractor, Tyrone leads you through a room-by-room survey of your marriage, revealing areas that may need attention, and explaining how you can repair, renew, refresh, and rebuild your relationship.

With humor, practical insights, and biblical wisdom, he provides the blueprint and the tools you need to build a marriage that honors God, blesses others, and fulfills your hopes.

Whatever the state of your marriage, it is never too late to turn it into a house of God's love.

Order Your Copy Today!

Contact the Author

Tyrone Holcomb
PO BOX 2542
Harker Heights, TX 76548

tholcomb@chop.org

Like us on Facebook
TyroneHolcomb

Follow us on twitter
@HolcombTyrone

Phone: (254) 547-1413